RELATIONAL REFUGEES

Relational Refugees

Alienation and Reincorporation in African American Churches and Communities

EDWARD P. WIMBERLY

Abingdon Press
Nashville

RELATIONAL REFUGEES
Alienation and Reincorporation in African American Churches and Communities

This book is printed on recycled, acid-free, elemental-chlorine-free paper.

Library of Congress Cataloging-in-Publication Data

Wimberly, Edward P., 1943–
    Relational refugees : alienation and reincorporation in African American churches and communities / Edward P. Wimberly.
       p. cm.
    Includes bibliographical references and index.
    ISBN 0-687-08798-8 (alk. paper)
      1. Mentoring in church work. 2. Interpersonal relations—Religious aspects—Christianity. 3. Church work with Afro-Americans. I. Title.
BV4408.5 .W56 2000
261.8'34896073—dc21

99-056508

00 01 02 03 04 05 06 07 08 09—10 9 8 7 6 5 4 3 2 1

MANUFACTURED IN THE UNITED STATES OF AMERICA

To all my students,
whom I have encouraged
in over twenty-four years
of teaching in theological seminaries

ACKNOWLEDGMENTS

In many ways bringing a manuscript to publication is a cooperative process. The idea for writing this book emerged while I was in Mutare, Zimbabwe, during a sabbatical at Africa University. I was able to find some of the literature I needed at Africa University, but many of the resources had to be sent or brought to me. James Salley, Assistant Vice Chancellor at Africa University, which has its headquarters in Nashville, graciously transported books to me. Dr. Henry Bilah, the Faculty of Humanities at Africa University, took the time from his busy schedule to read and make editorial comments on various drafts. I also e-mailed the manuscript to Archie Smith who made important comments that helped me shape the book.

When I returned from Zimbabwe, Robert Franklin, President of the Interdenominational Theological Center; faculty colleagues: Carolyn McCrary, Riggins Earl, and Joyce Guilory; my sister-in-law, Margaret Wimberly; my sister, Pam Jones; and my longtime colleague in the gospel, Gilbert H. Caldwell, read portions of the manuscript. Their comments proved most helpful and incorporating them into the text substanially improved it.

Many of my ideas about the village were shaped by a local congregation outside Mutare, Zimbabwe, called St. James United Methodist. Its pastor, Tiwirai Kufarimai, and Rev. and Mrs. Gift and Margaret Machinga helped me to envisage the significance of the local church in re-creating the village within the urban setting.

Although many people were instrumental in bringing about this project, the ideas expressed within are my responsibility. I am sure that those who read portions of the book will not agree with all the ideas I express. However, the feedback I received, especially on controversial issues, was invaluable.

The editorial staff of Abingdon Press was very helpful in making this project accessible to a wider audience. I am very appreciative of their help.

CONTENTS

CONTENTS

FOREWORD

Whenever we put pen to paper or fingertips to keyboard, we do so in a particular historical and cultural context. As I write this in July 1999 in Denver, Colorado, the newspaper and television reports serve to remind me almost daily of the tragedy that took place at Columbine High School in Littleton, Colorado. In that quiet suburb of Denver, not far from where I live or from the church where I am one of the pastors, two young men opened fire on their schoolmates.

That day, April 20, 1999 is etched in my memory not only because it occurred in my community but also for personal reasons. When news of the shootings and a possible hostage situation at the high school reached my church, I drove one of my colleagues, whose daughter teaches at the school, to Columbine. When we approached the campus, we were directed to a nearby elementary school where parents, teachers, and students gathered in the aftermath. It was an unforgettable scene.

In addition, I write these words mindful of Benjamin Smith who, on the weekend leading up to July 4, 1999, went on a shooting spree far from Denver, in Illinois and Indiana. Smith chose his victims because of their race or religion, reminding us all of the fragility of our national community. Violence, whether it takes place near or far, challenges our humanity, our faith, our political philosophy, and our sense of well-being.

In the text that follows, *Relational Refugees: Alienation and Reincorporation in African American Churches and Communities,* Edward P. Wimberly serves us well at this historical moment of anxiety, violence, and millennial change. He does this in two significant ways. First, he provides a new perspective on the inner cultural/historical/psychological refugee-reality of the African American community today. Sharing his profound spiritual and intellectual insights, Wimberly's exploration of the unique African American human experience utilizes, in a powerfully effective way, the fiction of a host of African American writers and scholars. His own spiritual insight and experience coupled with his demonstrated competence in pastoral counseling and psychology is evident as he opens before his readers, whether African American or not, the soul of a people who, even in this post-post–Civil Rights era, can still be characterized in the words of one preacher as America's "last and lost community."

Second, Ed Wimberly skillfully and effectively points to the universality of human experience. Instead of assuming that nothing of value to those of other cultural backgrounds can emerge from the experiences of African Americans, as tragically much of this nation still seems to believe, Wimberly, for those of us who have eyes to see, ears to hear, and hearts to respond, articulates wisdom from African American traditions that can inform and instruct persons in other communities. It was said of Jesus that nothing good could come out of Nazareth. Our society is not yet sure that the African American experience has anything to teach those beyond that experience and community. Yet, the young killers in Colorado and the young man who shot Jews, African Americans, and Koreans in Illinois fit well Wimberly's category of the "relational refugee." They, and those who might have stopped them from engaging in violence, may well have benefited from an understanding of African American alienation as Wimberly describes it. For example, if any community of persons knows something about disrespect (being "dissed") and how to manage the anger that erupts in response to both real and imagined moments of less than human respect, it is the African American community.

It is my hope that this book, which reflects the cumulative experiential and intellectual journey of Edward Wimberly, the author, and in this instance, the less visible but nevertheless evident companionship of his spouse, Anne S. Wimberly, will be a "cross-over" success. Musicians, whose idioms are drawn from a wide diversity of cultural contexts, are described as being "cross-over" artists. I hope that the lessons contained in this work will reach a world much larger than that of African American churches and communities.

The sermon that I preached on Sunday, July 4, 1999, was entitled "My Country 'tis of Thee." In it, I attempted to convey to the congregation at the predominantly white Park Hill United Methodist Church my affirmation of this nation despite my experience, and the experiences of my African American sisters and brothers, of racial discrimination in this "sweet land of liberty." I said:

> My "primary" ancestors, African Americans (although I now acknowledge other ancestry as well), were not at Plymouth Rock, either as members of the welcoming party or the landing party. Neither did they arrive at Ellis Island to be welcomed by the words of Emma Lazarus on the Statue of Liberty. Rather, my ancestors came on ships, not in first or tourist class, but below deck, most of the time in circumstances devestatingly inhumane. Nonetheless, "this is my country, land that I love."

So, too, I sense is Wimberly's hope—to be able to share with honest candor the experience and insight of my black sisters and brothers in this land and on Mother Africa, to express my hope and belief in the unrealized potential of this great nation. The late James Baldwin wrote:

> Every society is really governed by hidden laws, by unspoken but profound assumptions on the part of the people, and ours is no exception. It is up to the American writer to find out what these laws and assumptions are. In a society much given to smashing taboos without thereby managing to be liberated from them, it will be no easy matter.[1]

In his writings, Edward Wimberly shares with us stories of the human family who by virtue of race and circumstance are members of the African American village. But the stories of these African Americans speak to the experience of members of other villages as well. In fact, Wimberly's analysis shows, relational refugees are members of every village, no matter what that village looks like or how that village defines itself. And, further, their struggles, joys, sorrows, and dysfunction belong to all of us. Wimberly reminds us that that village needs mentors who will create and affect relationships that include rather than exclude, that love more than judge. We in the Christian "village" believe Creator/God gave us a Mentor/Savior in Jesus Christ. We seek to follow him.

There should be no debate about the historic and continuing woundedness of members of the African American community. Wimberly's work directly and indirectly communicates that our woundedness can be the source of healing within and beyond the African American community. African Americans are equipped to be the "wounded healer(s)" that Henri Nouwen describes so eloquently.

Wimberly's words smash taboos while at the same time he points to pathways of liberation that Baldwin reminds us are much harder to find. May the readers dare to claim them as their own!

Gilbert H. Caldwell

PREFACE

In January of 1998, while on sabbatical from the Interdenominational Theological Center my wife and I traveled to Africa University in Mutare, Zimbabwe. For the first three and a half months, we could do very little teaching, because we did not have work permits. Unfortunate as this delay was, it provided us with a great deal of time to get involved in the local community, and particularly in St. James United Methodist Church. We also had significant time to invest in reading and studying.

One book I read, which has had a lasting impact on me, was my colleague and longtime friend Archie Smith's *Navigating the Deep River*.[1] In this work, Smith explores the churches' deplorable treatment of homosexuals. He coins the term "spiritual refugees" to describe the situation of gay and lesbian Christians. Homosexuals are spiritual refugees because the churches refuse to offer them hospitality due to their sexual orientation. As I considered this idea of spiritual refugees, I quickly recognized that many types of people—homosexuals as well as other groups—suffer this same alienation. There are countless others who do not feel at home in the church or in the world and feel cut off from significant communities and relationships, who live as refugees outside the boundaries of the church.

Leaving the United States just two weeks after we buried my mother-in-law, my wife and I felt like refugees ourselves, suddenly ripped from our familiar surroundings and relationships. Yet, from the moment we stepped off the plane in Harare, Zimbabwe, we were embraced by a new community and made to feel at home.

Through our host and guide, a young woman named Nyasha Mawokomatanda, we were welcomed to Zimbabwe and into a new community that quickly came to feel like family. When Nyasha took us to St. James, her home church, we experienced a welcoming like no other in our lives. Within a matter of weeks, we were incorporated into a new family in an unfamiliar land, no longer refugees but pilgrims. We found a new home, a place to belong.

Being embraced immediately by a new community allowed us to probe more deeply into the differences between United States and Zimbabwean cultures. The contrast is striking. In the United States, we accept our alienation from community as normative and desirable. In Zimbabwe, it is the opposite. Our life in the United States, outside of our circle of immediate family and close friends, came to seem isolated and disconnected.

As I reflected both on our experience of this generous and immediate welcoming and on Smith's concept of the spiritual refugee, the idea for this book emerged. I decided that the concept of the refugee could be expanded so that it might contribute to the reestablishment of the village in the United States. The village, a close-knit and nurturing community, is essential to our pilgrimage in the world. In this book, I attempt to describe pathways toward a new village culture for those who feel alienated from community, and particularly from the local church.

In the United States the functions of the village have been divvied up among professional castes. The loss of nurturing community has resulted in the domination of the therapeutic model for emotional support. In Zimbabwe, the small village provides the essential relational and caring network that all people need to grow and develop into mature adults. With urbanization and modernity the village began to collapse. The caring functions diminished and became the work of specialized professional therapists and counselors. Thus, the dissolution of the village has contributed to the development of professional counseling and psychotherapy.

For our students at Africa University, the wisdom of the caring village was simply a part of their lives. Thus, our teaching began to focus on how to use the concepts of Western therapeutic theories to help our African students reflect on the caring wisdom and practices of the village. Our goal was not to replace traditional methods of healing but instead to encourage the students to preserve such

16

ideas and practices already alive in their local churches. At the same time, we used this experience to begin to develop an approach to pastoral care and counseling and to Christian education for African Americans. The pages that follow outline some ideas and practices that can help restore the communal caring resources of local congregations, drawn from the traditions of the villages of Zimbabwe and my own therapeutic paradigm—the reincorporation of relational refugees.

INTRODUCTION

After six months of pastoral counseling, Delores decided to end her counseling regimen. In my opinion, her decision to stop therapy was quite premature, but she insisted she was ready. She explained that she had reached her intended goal of gaining a better sense of self. I responded that she had just begun the process of true self-discovery and that she needed much more work in pastoral counseling. She disagreed.

Delores felt that she had gained new insight into the meaning of selfhood and so was prepared to get on with her life without my help. For her, selfhood meant detachment or withdrawal from participation in certain relationships. She understood the goal of life to be the ability of the self to stand alone and to rely totally on its own inner being for nurture and sustenance. Believing that this was an inadequate view of the self, I attempted to respond in ways that challenged her view of the self as autonomous. She remained unconvinced and eventually left not only the counseling relationship but also her marriage—her husband and her children.

Some women feel oppressed by marriage and motherhood and desire the freedom of singleness. This feeling often occurs at midlife. Delores's attempt to find her self by disengaging from the nurturing relationships in which she participated was self-destructive. In fact, this was confirmed by her subsequent behavior. She got involved in a very destructive relationship with another man, which undermined the autonomy she had obtained in therapy. It was clear to me that she had cut herself off from relationships that were more nurturing than the ones she eventually attained.

When she began her counseling, Delores was struggling with her commitment to marriage and family because she had been sexually molested at an early age. This experience became the focal point of how she felt about herself. When she left her husband and children, the unresolved issues related to her molestation began slowly to surface. Having never resolved the violation of trust in intimate relationships as a child, Delores found herself adrift as an adult.

Because of deeply held religious beliefs, George struggled profoundly to overcome his homosexual tendency. He desired intimacy but his self-loathing served as an insurmountable barrier. Unlike Delores, George desperately desired to be in wholesome relationships with others, but found this impossible to achieve. Reared by a mother and father who were emotionally unavailable for him, George sought connection with others in anonymous phone sex and occasional genital interaction with same-sex partners. These unsatisfying encounters only increased his self-loathing, shame, and alienation from others. He felt completely unlovable and despaired over the prospect of ever finding someone who could really care for him. The more despair he felt, the more he pursued anonymous sexual relationships.

Delores and George are what I have come to call "relational refugees." Relational refugees are persons not grounded in nurturing and liberating relationships. They are detached and without significant connections with others who promote self-development. They lack a warm relational environment in which to define and nurture their self-identity. As a consequence, they withdraw into destructive relationships that exacerbate rather than alleviate their predicament.

Relational refugees, such as Delores and George, can be found throughout contemporary society, a society shaped in significant ways by the historical circumstances known as modernity. *Modernity* is the term used to characterize our life together as influenced by the technological and scientific advances of the last two centuries and the accompanying philosophical and ideological shifts in thinking.[1] One such ideological emphasis is the belief that self-actualization involves cultivating autonomy. Such a view, carried to the extreme, results in the belief and conviction that being a self comes from being disengaged from significant relationships and standing completely alone.

The understanding of the self in modernity is affected by advances in technology, which leads to further discoveries and more technology and still newer selves. The computer, for instance, has become central in the lives of many of us. Computers ease many tasks but also change the form and quality of human relationships. Recently computers have made it possible to experience what is called virtual reality. We can now participate in relationships without the constraints of our enfleshed selves, our genetic dispositions, and our socioeconomic characteristics, but instead as self-created beings. As a cartoonist has put it, the Internet is great because as I type at the keyboard "no one but me knows I'm a dog." In this context, we come to believe we can achieve selfhood by disengaging from embodied relationships. In virtual reality, real life is lived outside of relationships and the pain associated with them.

Living in virtual reality we come to imagine that it is possible to be a self while avoiding pain and suffering. Human beings have desired to live lives free of pain and suffering since the beginning of time. The biblical stories of creation narrate the consequences of this desire. The modern striving for autonomy is simply the latest manifestation of this human desire. The crisis of personality and identity that is a result of withdrawing from nurturing relationships and relying solely on the self creates a form of homelessness, which I identify as relational refugeeism.

Delores and George are relational refugees. They have withdrawn from relationships and pursued a life of autonomy. They have destroyed the webs of support they need to cultivate a positive sense of self and, as a result, are incapable of healthy relationships with those who surround them.

The purposes of this book are (1) to define the meaning of the term *relational refugee;* (2) to identify means to heal relational refugees and restore them to nurturing relationships that will enable them to become whole, liberated selves; (3) to suggest that the formation of mentoring relationships is a major vehicle for achieving liberated selfhood; (4) to explore various social issues that affect relational refugees, and through those issues the larger society—issues such as violence, domestic strife, adolescent identity development, attitudes toward money, grandparenting, drug addiction, and dying with dignity; and (5) to highlight the contribution of African American churches, which have a tradition of supporting mentoring relationships.

Relational Refugees

Archie Smith observes that there are many people who share the common characteristics of "being uprooted, homeless, and landless; seeking shelter in another place; losing the protection of one's rights; imprisonment; and deportation."[2] He calls these persons refugees, displaced in the sense of being forcibly removed from their customary place by oppressive forces.

I extend Smith's concept of refugees here. While I desire to maintain Smith's emphasis on the ways in which many are forced into homelessness, my concern is with those who have been deceived by society into thinking that cutting themselves off from family, community, and past generations will lead to growth and life enhancement.[3] In other words, my term relational refugees refers to those who have become homeless primarily because they have cut themselves off from community, the community of the living and of the ancestors.

Peter Berger and his colleagues discuss the types of persons I am interested in as those who suffer from a homeless mind.[4] Berger is interested in the ways people use images from social and economic life to shape their self-identity. One such image equates the self with a machine. This image compartmentalizes life into private and public spheres, detaching self from feelings. People whose dominant self-image is that of a computer construct virtual worlds. These worlds encourage withdrawal from, rather than engagement in, nurturing relationships. To live as a computer is to live as a refugee.

Relational refugees, to my mind, have not been forced into this situation of homelessness. Instead, they are fleeing former relationships in the pursuit of what they consider higher values. Perhaps the relationships in which they were involved did not produce the kinds of rewards that they have come to expect. Whether pursuing wealth or status or some other dream, relational refugees suddenly find themselves adrift in life without an anchor or a life jacket. They often do not even recognize their emotional homelessness, but continue to live stoically without support from past generations and traditions.

Restoring Nurturing Relationships

I contend relational refugees need to restore for themselves nurturing relationships that can address their emotional needs. In this book, I offer strategies for relational refugees, and those who seek to assist them, to re-create a community context in which they can live more wholly. There are certain kinds of relationships that emotional refugees need to enter in order to help them become full participants in life and to achieve liberated selfhood.

Relational refugees need positive relationships with one or more individuals whose attitudes they can internalize. Human beings need to be surrounded by people who have positive attitudes toward them, because such attitudes become the basis for one's own positive self-image. People become selves by internalizing the attitudes of others.

George's self-loathing centered on his parent's aloofness and his feeling of homelessness after his family moved when he was five years old, due to his father's military transfer. He has never found friends or felt at home in the world since then. To heal, George needs simultaneously to come to some measure of self-acceptance and to counter the painful legacy of his upbringing by finding a strong network of support. George needs to enter an apprenticeship of love and nurture with a trustworthy friend or mentor who can lead him back to human community and companionship. In the context of positive relationship, George would learn to give and receive nurture as a way to counteract the negative messages he had previously internalized.

Human beings learn to live in a healthy, whole manner by seeing such practices demonstrated by others they trust, imitating these patterns and rehearsing their own ways of living. Such experiences form internalized scenarios that govern how people interpret subsequent experiences. If people internalize only negative experiences, they will develop negative scenarios, which then become patterns of response to later experiences, whether positive or negative. Delores, for example, was sexually molested at the age of eleven. She had internalized this experience, and it became the dominant filter for interpreting her subsequent relationships. When her daughter reached the age of eleven, the negative scene took center stage. Unable to cope with the pain of the resurfacing memories, Delores withdrew from her husband and children. But Delores could not heal her pain by withdrawing. Instead, she needed to participate in nurturing relationships that could provide positive patterns to counteract the negative ones that haunted her.

Human beings also develop a positive self-understanding by adopting and identifying with positive narratives and roles through which they can orient their lives. Such narratives and roles are provided by caring communities and mentors. George and Delores were both on the periphery of faith communities that were constituted by such narratives. Scripture serves, among other things, as a collection of stories onto which we graft our own story. Faith communities provide in their stories and role models support for our journeys toward relational homes and liberated selves.

Unfortunately, neither Delores nor George was ready to participate in the faith communities available to them because of negative experiences in earlier stages of their lives. Delores, for example, had become involved in church life but became sexually involved with the minister. The sexual dimension of this relationship revived her memories of being sexually molested as a child. As a consequence, her church became for her another negative space. Instead of sanctuary, her church was simply another unsafe place. To return she needed careful treatment. Delores needed to experience safe and nurturing relationships before she could ever trust the church community again. Such relationships had to be warm and caring with the sexual boundaries clearly established. Pastoral counseling is often a place where such care is found.

George also found churches alienating rather than hospitable. He attended church quite frequently, but felt he would be rejected if people knew of his sexual orientation. His self-loathing prevented him from engaging people in the church, and this feeling was exacerbated when there were negative remarks about homosexuality from the pulpit. At such times, George would flee from the church to pursue his life of desperation. He needed to internalize more positive attitudes about himself before he could take the risk of entering fully into a mainstream church community where he would have to endure the pervasive suspicions about homosexuals. However, neither did he see himself becoming a member of a church that was predominantly for homosexuals. He needed to internalize more positive attitudes before he could avail himself of the narratives and roles provided by the faith community. Again, pastoral counseling would be a prerequisite for his participation in a church.

The African American Church and Mentoring

Pastoral counseling can assist in the reintegration of relational refugees into nurturing communities. The techniques and concerns of pastoral counseling are important resources for the process of healing. However, there is an indigenous model of ministry in African American churches that can also facilitate the healing and wholeness of the emotional refugee. African American faith communities have long practiced and supported mentoring relationships that foster individual growth and self-actualization.

Mentoring relationships in African American communities of faith facilitate the adoption of positive attitudes, scenes, narratives, and roles. For example, at a later date, George joined a church. He began to develop close friendships with men who he found maintained firm sexual boundaries. He felt secure with these men who did not wish to enter a sexual relationship with him. These relationships began to form the basis for him to learn new patterns of living.

I believe pastoral counseling is a first step in the reincorporation of relational refugees. The counseling can help the refugee move toward full participation in the faith community. However, the African American church with its tradition of mentoring relationships is an additional model for those who seek to create the kind of caring environment where the relational refugee can feel at home and grow.

Consequently, this book is not intended solely for African Americans. The church as a whole needs to address the needs of the relational refugee. This book is thoroughly grounded in the experience of the African American community and church, but I hope its insights will speak to others who experience related but distinct forms of alienation and yearning for community. After all, members of all cultural groups experience themselves as relational refugees.

The Context of African American Mentoring

In describing the tradition of mentoring, I take seriously the context of the African American community. African Americans live as a minority within North American society. Although we have a legacy and heritage of values and traditions of our own, rooted in Africa and in our creative adaptation of Christian traditions in response to slavery and its legacy of racism, we still live within a society that has dominant values that affect our lives. What drives this book is the awareness that there are certain values of dominant society, which we cannot escape, that influence our various levels of mentoring.[5]

The clash between our historic spiritual values and the dominant cultural values can be seen clearly in some of the current movies and documentaries that treat African American themes. For example, in the stimulating and action-packed movie *Hoodlum,* the characters struggle to prevent the encroachment of the white mob on the underworld activity of the African American community. In this context, violence is used to protect the black community from this invasion. The movie focuses on the limitations of the use of violence to achieve certain worthwhile values, and demonstrates that violence may not be the best strategy to pursue.

Hoodlum addresses a dominant theme of the wider North American society, the redemptive use of violence.[6] Whereas resorting to violence may sometimes be a necessity in an imperfect world, in the history of the United States African Americans have been on the receiving end more often than not. Although not unanimous by any stretch, the African American community has determined, as Audre Lorde has said, "the master's tools will never dismantle the master's house."[7] The point is that what we learn and do as African Americans is influenced greatly by the wider context in which we live. In mentoring, it is necessary to examine what directions are provided by the wider social value system and how these directives support or conflict with the values embedded in our spiritual heritage.

This book attempts to identify the relationship between individual alienation and some of the major issues confronting the African American community today. I contend that many problems have roots in the deterioration of nurturing communities throughout our society and that solutions to these problems rest ultimately on the re-creation of a village culture. Mentors are needed to help relational refugees reintegrate themselves into the community. The role of the mentor also includes identifying the wider social values that shape the context in which this process of healing occurs. Helping to modify the negative influence of these wider societal values and facilitating the use of the spiritual and religious legacy of the learner are additional tasks of African American mentors.

Relational refugees are all alone, trying to find their way in the world. They feel abandoned by significant others as they try to sort out what is valuable and important. Mentors help immensely in this process of meaning making. With mentors as guides, relational refugees become *pilgrims,* who are able to feel at home in the world, to participate in the life of a significant faith community, to engage in a purposeful and meaningful future.

A Forward Look

In the chapters that follow, I discuss examples of social conflicts that are rooted in the breakdown of community. I propose throughout that African American mentoring traditions can help us solve these problems by creating for refugees a meaningful place and home in the world. There are many forces that would make us homeless in the world. This book seeks to address these forces and dynamics of homelessness.

Chapter 1 outlines a model of mentoring based on African American indigenous practical rationality. Mentors teach relational refugees new patterns of living that nurture the individual and draw her or him back into the community. The African American model addresses all aspects of life and, through imitation and identification, inculcates not only new behaviors but an entire worldview.

Each subsequent chapter will examine important issues related to relational refugees. I draw upon my pastoral counseling experience but also upon examples of African American literature and other media to examine the dimensions of these issues. In chapter 2, I address violence. Chapter 3 focuses on animosity in black male-female relationships. Chapter 4 examines the pain of adolescent identity. Chapter 5 addresses the stress of limited economic opportunity. Chapter 6 explores issues related to grandparents who serve as substitute parents. Chapter 7 explores the role of surrogate fathers in African American families. In chapter 8, I discuss issues of death and dying.

In the conclusion, I suggest ways in which African American churches and seminaries, like small villages, can provide models of relationships that nurture and support the liberated selfhood of their members.

RELATIONAL REFUGEES

CHAPTER ONE

A MODEL FOR PASTORAL CARE: AFRICAN AMERICAN MENTORING

We live in a society that produces, at an alarming rate, relational refugees, people disconnected from significant relationships, people like Delores and George. Finding ways to minister to the needs of relational refugees is an essential task.

In *Another Day's Journey*, Robert Franklin, president of the Interdenominational Theological Center, relates how he used to walk across the Morehouse College campus listening to tapes of great black preachers and reading the poetry of outstanding black poets. These times of quiet contemplation in conversation with great wordsmiths shaped his approach to preaching.[1] Many other African preachers can attest to similar ways of learning their craft, of learning to preach by internalizing the styles and techniques of others as they came to discover their own style. At the time, some criticized such activity for promoting the use of gimmicks to fit into the black preaching tradition. I now want to reclaim the practical rationality that is involved in the process of learning to preach by listening to one's elders, one example of the traditions of African American mentoring.

Just as Franklin found his own voice by listening to the preaching of others, African Americans transmit our cultural heritage through oral tradition and apprentice-like relationships. I call these techniques of cultural transmission "mentoring" relationships and seek in this chapter to outline the structures of such relationships that transmit skills not only for professional ministry but for all aspects of life.

Relational refugees need to learn how to live in relationships. It

31

is through mentoring relationships that they can begin to heal, to reenter the human community. African American church leaders have generally learned these skills by being brought up in a context of nurturing relationships themselves. Certainly African American culture can offer these skills to the wider society. Wherever relational refugees exist, such relationships can and should be established.

African Americans employ mentoring relationships to transmit a variety of skills and to help people develop into mature and productive members of the community. Mentoring is, in fact, a model for transmiting life skills and can serve as the basis for theological education and pastoral care ministries. In situations that involve relational refugees, the mentoring model is especially helpful. Mentors can serve relational refugees as a bridge back into community, a means to overcome their feelings of homelessness. Mentors help relational refugees cultivate a worldview that orients them in terms of their self-identity, their membership in community, and their place in the world.

Relational Practical Rationality

Theologians and other church leaders tend to separate theological reflection from practical application of such theory, giving priority to the former. Some even claim that theological reflection is authentic only when it is structured according to Western logic, technical jargon, and linear rationality. Theological reflection based on mentoring relationships is thought to be inferior because it involves imitation rather than critical thinking. Consequently, the tradition of exuberant, celebrative preaching, the creative turn of phrase, and indulgence in metaphorical logic is relegated to an inferior status. In reaction, most African American preaching professors have emphasized content preaching, scorning techniques of dramatic and creative delivery.

Fortunately, people like Robert Franklin, and others now acknowledged as great preachers, found a way to appropriate the traditions of black preaching along with a form of rationality that had integrity. They have begun to restore the dignity of other ways of teaching and learning. Yet, I do not think we have fully grasped the significance of the way we, as African American preachers and ministers, go about thinking—about how we combine scientific rationality with metaphorical and narrative modes of thought in all we do.

African American pastors have not only learned to preach by copying and internalizing the styles of their mentors, they have also learned other skills for ministry through imitation. Elsewhere, I have called these modes of transmission indigenous learning.[2] While this way of learning has sometimes been ridiculed within academic circles, it is time to reclaim and revalue this significant way of knowing and doing that is fundamental to African American practical theology and, in fact, to African American community life.

Those of us involved in preparing African American students for ministry understand much better today the basic ways the African American community has traditionally gone about learning and making meaning. To increase our effectiveness in ministry, it is important that those of us who teach the theological arts to African Americans and members of other ethnic groups become better acquainted with indigenous styles of learning and mentoring so that these styles can be more fully appropriated, developed, and understood.

Mentoring as Mimetic Activity

Mentoring is a relational style of teaching. Mentors make themselves available to help students, congregants, and neighbors develop the skills for living in relationship. Among relational refugees, mentors help those who feel homeless find an emotional, relational, spiritual, and cognitive home. Mentoring has sometimes been limited to those who serve as role models for younger people, helping them perform vital and socially sanctioned functions in society. For me, mentoring includes the wider function of assisting relational refugees to overcome the emotional, relational, spiritual, and cognitive alienation that they feel in the world.

To be a mentor is to teach by example. To be mentored is to follow an example, to imitate. The word *imitate* derives from the older term *mimesis*. Black practical theologians, such as Romney Moseley and Archie Smith, engage in what they call mimetic theory to describe this process of social formation.[3] Moseley and Smith both discuss ministry as "repeating acts of love." They highlight ministry as repetition or reenactment of specific acts of caring.[4] In their works, they outline the rudiments of a basic theory of mimesis, a form of relational practical rationality.[5]

Mimetic theory allows us to expand our definition of mentoring. Connecting familiar forms of teaching with a larger discussion of social formation, we begin to see mentoring as a form of learning that can heal those who find themselves relational refugees. In a strong relationship with a skilled mentor or mentors, relational refugees are drawn back into nurturing community and are enabled to develop a healthy sense of self in the context of others. Mimetic theory outlines some of the specific forms in which this growth takes place. Mentors and the traditions they draw upon provide a new understanding of self in relation to a social order that draws the refugee back into community. There are several levels on which this learning takes place simultaneously. These include: myths and stories that contain *plots* in which the refugee can locate him or herself, *roles* that offer new patterns of behavior, *scenes* that convey how the refugee might respond in various social situations, and *attitudes* that can make alternative responses to various circumstances possible.

Through stories, we learn to be selves and to act in certain ways. Through roles, we discover healthy ways to interact with others. Through repeating scenes, we rehearse our responses to new situations. Through internalizing the attitudes of others, we grow in emotional maturity. Mentoring is a form of practical rationality in which the mentor teaches by example, in addition to advising and questioning. Those being mentored internalize these holistic and embodied lessons as they begin to make sense out of who they are and how they will participate in life.

Mentoring is a process of ordering experiences, giving priority to certain stories, scenes, roles, and attitudes.[6] The mentor must communicate which perspectives and traditions are most legitimate for the healthy development of an individual grounded in community. Such privileging enables the construction of a meaningful world where students, learners, and disciples feel at home and function as responsible members of society.

Mentoring Skills

Relational refugees, like all human beings, need to be connected and related significantly to others. Only by living in relationship can we discover our true identities, our roles, and the purpose and meaning of our lives. If we cut ourselves off from meaningful relationships, we become vulnerable to meaninglessness, strangers to the world.

Alienation is what relational refugees feel in the world. Many churches contribute to, rather than alleviate, this feeling of alienation because they communicate certain exclusive attitudes. Sometimes ministers and others within churches are abusive mentors and exploit the vulnerabilities of relational refugees. Thus, relational refugees often find churches unsafe and unhelpful in their journey toward wholeness.

Worthy mentors, skilled mentors, and compassionate mentors are needed to enable relational refugees to return home. Mentors with character and compassion can enable relational refugees to find new stories, scenes, roles, and attitudes to replace the negative stories and experiences that are the underlying causes of their alienation.

In contemporary culture, where mentoring traditions are difficult to pass from one generation to the next, the skills of mentoring must be made explicit and taught. Therefore, it is important to identify and explicate the skills that we need to teach.

There are certain skills that the mentor employs to assist persons to feel at home in the world. One such skill is called *phenomenological attending*. Phenomenological attending is a way of being available to the learner. It is the use of caring empathy to attend to the experiences, images, metaphors, narratives, ideas, and concepts of relational refugees. Here the mentor seeks to connect with the learner's deepest feelings and experiences. Through empathetic listening the mentor provides a safe space for the refugee to risk attempting a human connection which is basic if she or he is to come to feel at home in the world. The mentor invites the learner to imitate the mentor's positive attitude and way of being present. This communicates welcoming hospitality. When she or he accepts the mentor's hospitality, the learner is no longer homeless.

Once trust is established and the learner's story has been drawn out, the mentor helps the learner explore in depth the images, metaphors, narratives, and ideas that emerged in the attending phase. This further extends hospitality and validates the learner's experiences. This attention also helps the learner examine the significant dimensions of his or her experiences and focus on those which are health promoting. It is the health promoting experience that enables the learner to identify and move beyond her or his negative scenes of rejection and alienation. The mentor can help the learner sort through the stories, plots, and roles, identifying those that build the learner's self-esteem and sense of worth. Thus, the mentor is a guide whom the learner follows to reinterpret his or her experiences in health producing ways.

As a guide, the mentor also helps point the learner to what is valuable and worthwhile. The relational refugee tends to be an expert in devaluing himself or herself, internalizing those negative messages that abound in society. The mentor, conversely, facilitates the learner's identification with what the mentor deems valuable and worthwhile. It is through identification with what the mentor values that the learner learns to value himself or herself, others, institutions, and a variety of other things. Through this identification with and internalization of the mentor's values the learner discovers the meaning of character and a way to be ethically and morally present in the world. In a real way, mentoring is a formation process through which the learner develops character, identity, values, self-worth, and a way of being in the world. In short, mentoring is a holistic process encompassing all the dimensions of personhood.

The mentor not only develops skills, but also a code of conduct for guiding the application of these skills. There are certain ethical standards that must be maintained at all times to facilitate optimum mentoring. Such ethical standards include power and boundary issues. For example, under no circumstances should the mentor use his or her position, power, or authority to exploit the mentoring relationship for personal reward or gain, such as financial gain or sexual favors. Creating and maintaining secure boundaries in the mentoring relationship is absolutely mandatory since the betrayal of trust is often a crucial piece of the refugee's story. On the practical level, this means the mentor should establish a schedule of regular appointments and limit contact with the learner to those scheduled appointments.

Mentors need not only to work in an intense way on the particular experiences of the individual, but also give direct attention to social conditions and values that contribute to the individual's situation. Such multitiered analysis should happen not only in the therapeutic realm but in the larger sphere of social discourse as well. When the mentor attends to issues and values that produce and foster relational refugee status, the mentor becomes a public theologian. A public theologian uses public forums to identify and criticize the conditions that help create relational refugees in the first place.

As public theologians, mentors need to tackle some of the major issues confronting the African American community today, including identifying the wider social values that shape the context in which mentoring occurs. Modifying the negative influence of wider societal values is an important aspect of the work of mentors interested in transforming not only individual lives but the culture in which they live.

The Justification of Practical Rationality

Models of ministry based on relational practical rationality and mentoring have roots in the origins of our traditions. In fact, I would argue, they are basic to our faith. From the very beginning of Christianity, church leaders showed their interest in enabling people to grow in the faith.[7] Converts to Christianity have always been expected to be transformed, to develop and grow, in light of the new understanding that faith brought to them.

Our Scriptures take for granted certain forms of mentoring. For example, Paul expected his followers to imitate him just as he imitated Christ. He thought of himself as an excellent model for others to follow.[8] Members of the Body of Christ follow a path that Jesus first traveled, a path that ends in the already, not yet reality of the kingdom of God. As we journey, saints, both those officially recognized and the many local heroes and heroines of faith, rise up for us to emulate.

To be human means to grow and to develop. Both our physical growth and development and our emotional and intellectual maturation are influenced by the geographical, linguistic, social, and cultural context in which we live. There was a time when we took for granted the context in which we live without analyzing or determining whether it was helpful to our growth. However, more recent philosophical perspectives have revealed the extent of the influence of the cultural context on individual development and often contain the suspicion that the contexts in which we are formed are *not* always helpful to us. For instance, African Americans, as they come to maturity, must contend with the cultural forces of white supremacy. To arrive at self-acceptance and patterns of behavior that are socially responsible, while fighting racist assaults, is both difficult and rewarding. Thus, exploring the dynamic forces that have shaped our lives has become an important part of modern and postmodern perspectives. The identification of a subject's social location has become the new common sense. Scholars now regularly explore the social, cultural and linguistic forces that have shaped our lives.[9] These methods of analysis have made clear that not only do individuals grow and develop but cultures and societies do as well. Mentors who can attend not only to the growth of the individual, but to shifts in the context in which such growth takes place, are all the more necessary now.

Like faith development, theological education also is based upon a fundamental belief that people grow and change. It is the job of theological education to mentor people through the change process. Whereas theological education today often utilizes traditional didactic pedagogies, mentoring or apprenticing models also exist. In many black churches where a master's degree is less important than a performance-based demonstration of one's call and one's anointing by the Spirit, skills gained through mentoring relationships have been primary in ministerial development. Whereas these traditions are not without their critics, their strengths commend them to our attention once again.

African American Christianity is a particular trajectory of the larger tradition that has emphasized the liberative themes of Scripture and has fostered a legacy of protest against social and economic oppression. Understanding viscerally that God is involved in struggles for freedom and justice, African American Christians have always thought of ministry in terms of transformation of persons and society. Consequently, African American ministry has a long history of practical and liberating rationality on which the mentor can draw.

Christianity, as a living faith, produces change, t
change that relational practical rationality and mentorin
to produce. Christians are called to get involved in God's
mation of the world. Our task, as practical theologians a
tors, then, is to build on an ancient and modern tradition o. thinking about ministry in ways that bring transformation.

From Refugee to Liberated Growth

In the chapters that follow, I address specific issues using the
model of mentoring developed in this chapter. Writers of fiction
are often our most skillful cultural observers. Recognizing this, I
use various novels and plays to shed light on situations that produce relational refugees and the accompanying problems associated with being alienated from the community. It is my contention that the alienation people feel generates many of the social
problems that we confront today, such as violence, addiction,
domestic abuse, and dysfunctional parenting. I draw some of these
connections to emphasize again the importance of looking beyond
the particular story of the individual to the larger context, in order
to produce lasting change in the refugee and in the culture. The
ultimate goal of the mentoring relationship must be as grand as
God's promises—the growth of the person into a whole, liberated
self, able to live responsibly and productively in the midst of a just
and peaceful world.

CHAPTER TWO

VIOLENCE AND
THE RELATIONAL
REFUGEE

Responding to the televised documentary drama called *The Edmond Perry Story,* the nation seemed completely baffled that a promising young black teen could end up dead by the bullet of a plainclothes police officer. To many in the African American community the tragic incident was a reminder of racism's ugly presence. To many whites, who believed that the American dream could be a reality for all, Edmond's death pierced their blind optimism. There was profound disbelief and confusion among many. In my case, I began to look at various scenes in the documentary to find the answer to my own queries about Edmond's tragic and untimely death. My questioning led beyond a superficial blaming of racism. I wanted to know exactly how racism was involved in Edmond's situation. I certainly agreed that racism was involved, but I had to find out how and why and explore the many subtle and diverse ways that racism manifested itself.

The reasons that Edmond came to a violent end are not obvious. Of course, racism was a factor, but a facile and reckless charge of racism as the only and sufficient cause not only removes the personal responsibility from those who choose to use violence but also trivializes the meaning of the word *racism.*

Edmond used and ultimately was a victim of violence, at least in part because he was a relational refugee. Thus, the goal of this chapter is to describe how he became a relational refugee and how mentoring might help those who turn to violence, as a response to their sense of alienation, choose alternative behaviors.

The Story of Edmond Perry

Edmond grew up in Harlem. He was a gifted and promising student. His teacher and mother were aware of his academic gifts and decided he needed a better intellectual environment than the New York City public school system could offer. They felt fortunate to find him a scholarship that enabled him to attend an exclusive and predominantly white preparatory school in New Hampshire. However, Edmond was not ready to be uprooted from his family and his community. Moreover, he was not ready for the impersonal atmosphere and indifference of the new school. He could not fit in. Soon he began to realize that his skin color was a major factor in his frequent experiences of rejection by his classmates.

One day, at home in Harlem, he encountered the same indifference he felt at the exclusive preparatory school, according to the televised documentary. Edmond had just finished playing basketball with his brother near his home in Harlem. A plainclothes white policeman was pursuing a suspect he had staked out. He passed by Edmond and his brother as if his mind were somewhere else. Edmond was incensed by what he thought was the plainclothes policeman's attitude toward him. He pursued the policeman and attacked him. During the struggle, the policeman shot and killed Edmond.

Of course, it was Edmond who interpreted the apparent indifference of the policeman in light of what he had been experiencing at the prep school. As a consequence of this interpretation Edmond felt the flush of humiliation. He felt he had been disrespected. He ran after the plainclothes policeman. When he caught the policeman, he jumped him and began to beat him. The policeman, fearing for his life, drew his gun and shot Edmond to death.

The Meaning of Violence

Edmond's story helps us grasp the relationship between the predicament of relational refugees and violence. By violence, I mean the use of physical force such as kicking, biting, punching, beating, shaking, shoving, stabbing, and shooting by one person with the intent of causing harm to another. I do not mean violence to include threats of violence or mere temper tantrums, unless a potential victim is prevented from exiting the situation or if the verbal threats immobilize or terrorize the victim into inaction for fear of physical assault.

To physically harm another person is always difficult to justify but at the same time must be seen in its social context in order to be fully understood. In other words, there is a contextual aspect to the meaning of violence. For instance, when an African American commits an act of violence, the act is often a means of striking out in a defensive manner to protect the inner self from feelings of devaluation.[1] It is the sense of feeling devalued that helps link violence to the concept of the relational refugee.

Edmond Perry's explanation of his use of violence unfolds as the documentary proceeds. The screenwriter places these words in his mouth right before the fatal scene: "I can be disrespected at the school I attend, but I won't be disrespected in my own community." The filmmaker seems to imply that Edmond could and did expect to be treated differently in his home community than in the white world where he spent his school days. But the plainclothes detective made him feel as ignored and rejected in his own territory, as he did in New Hampshire. Edmond could not accept this.

Edmond as a Relational Refugee

Edmond Perry's refugee status helps to explain his level of frustration. The opportunity to attend an exclusive private white school and to escape the so-called inferior ghetto schools of the inner city was seen by his mother and teachers as his ticket out of the cycle of poverty, to fulfillment of the American dream. Without being aware of the multiple barriers set up to block a young black man's success, they sent Edmond away with high hopes. Perhaps they did not realize what being uprooted from one's familiar roots could do to someone who was not ready for such an experience. Edmond became a relational refugee the moment he was prematurely uprooted from his home.

Edmond discovered quickly that the roles he could play at this exclusive white private school were limited to well-known racial stereotypes. First, he was encouraged by his white friends to go out for the basketball team, even though he was not a good basketball player. Next, when he tried his hand at interracial dating, he received only harsh and decisive rejections. Finally, he joined a fraternity of nerds thinking that they could not possibly reject him, but found that they accepted him as a member in hopes that he would use his Harlem drug connections for their benefit.

Understandably, Edmond was devastated and on the brink of despair. He struck back at his rejection through reliance on physical violence. He was suspended from school for resorting to violence. His naive optimism disappeared. He concluded that he simply would never fit in.

The lack of interpersonal bonds generates or activates deep feelings of humiliation in all people. In turn, these feelings may cause us to strike out in violence if we do not imagine any other way to reestablish community. Relational refugees who really have no positive roots in supportive, caring, communities often turn to the use of violence as a desperate statement about their unacknowledged emotional and relational homelessness.

How could a look of indifference trigger feelings of humiliation to the extent that Edmond would turn violent? His flawed thinking and interpretation of indifference as an insult led to his death. Edmond's effort to respond to the perceived insult put him in harm's way.

Cultural Values and Violence

The use of violence to redress humiliation and shame is often tacitly approved of within a cultural system. This was true in the ancient world and at certain points in United States history as well. In other words, there are precedents that exist which sanction the use of violence to recover the dignity one has lost owing to the acts of others.

Biblical scholar Robert Jewett explores in his book, entitled *Saint Paul Returns to the Movies,* the meaning of violence in contemporary films. He gives particular attention to the movie *Deliverance*.[2] In that movie, violence is used to restore the honor of a man who has been humiliated and abused by two other men. The hero of the film does not pursue the men to bring them to justice, but instead to mete out his own punishment upon them. Jewett understands the movie as a justification for the use of violence to restore the honor and dignity of someone who has lost theirs. From Jewett's perspective, the use of violence to redeem a person from shame and humiliation is deeply embedded in the fabric of life in the United States, as well as in ancient Mediterranean society.

In a similar way, I believe that Edmond attempted to redeem himself from humiliation when he resorted to violence. He apparently thought violence was an appropriate means to redress grievances.

Shame and Violence

In my view, Edmond's major grievance was not against this particular policeman, but was instead rooted in deep feelings of shame. Shame erupts when those important to us reject us as inadequate. Shame involves the total self. Its power is inescapable. It deals a severe and devastating blow to our sense of self-worth. We experience the rejection as a loss of love, as confirmation of our own assessment that we are ultimately unacceptable. Such blows to our self-esteem can trigger a desire for revenge against those who inflicted the shame on us. Violence explodes when the feelings of revenge are combined with the notion that it is possible to redeem the self from shame through violence, or rather that there is no course other than violence open to us.[3]

There is also a racial dimension in the use of violence to redeem the self from shame. Historically, whites have inflicted violence on blacks as a means of confirming their own self-worth, and racist structures of justice have protected many perpetrators from accountability. Growing up in the North in the 1950s, I remember vividly the killing of Emmett Till by whites for apparently whistling at a white woman. Whereas any man whistling at a woman today might be seen as guilty of sexual harassment, even in those more permissive days Emmett's punishment did not fit his so-called crime. His killers handed out a death penalty without a trial. Indeed, they used violence to restore the dignity of a white woman who had been insulted by a black male. And they got away with it. In other words, the use of violence to redeem the self from shame is permitted by the larger society but only for members of certain groups under specific circumstances. In no case would blacks be allowed to use violence to redeem themselves from insults by whites. The very thought of such a thing happening would outrage most whites. Blacks who have sought to restore their honor and integrity through violence have felt the full wrath of the so-called white justice system. The musical *Ragtime* illustrates this dilemma forcefully.

Relational refugees resort to violence predictably. People who have fragile connections with others become dangerous when they lose hope of escaping their isolation and sink into a raging despair. When relational refugees link their feelings of humiliation, they sometimes identify an individual or group to blame for their predicament. They can then justify their use of violence as revenge upon those who have caused their shame. They know that others have justified their actions in the same way. They have seen similar plots played out in the culture around them. They draw on the tradition of violent self-redemption and lash out.

Identification and Pastoral Care of the Enraged

In the predominantly white prep school, Edmond did not find a mentor to help him deal with his isolation and rejection. Instead, Edmond found himself surrounded by uncaring and exploitative people. Nurturing persons seemed absent.

Edmond needed a mentor, a nurturing relational presence. He needed someone to model for him a different attitude, one that would help him counteract the negative sentiments he had internalized. Through the internalization of a mentor's positive attitude, Edmond would have possessed an additional resource for choosing a course of action other than violence. The role, then, of the mentor is to intervene in the life of the relational refugee, to enable more constructive responses to life situations.

Edmond was not compelled to use violence in response to his situation of being uprooted and ashamed. However, he did. Perhaps he simply could envision no option besides violence in his way of interpreting reality.

Anyone who has deep feelings of shame faces the same choice that Edmond did. They can choose violence, but there are other options. There does appear to be a close connection between the desperation associated with losing love and affection and the use of violence. The option for violence seems to be chosen when those involved feel helplessly abandoned by others.

Being a relational refugee does not excuse the choices Edmond made, however. He chose poorly in terms of his treatment of the policeman, and clearly for himself, as well. It does appear that there may have been intervention possibilities that might have prevented his use of violence. It is precisely the job of the mentor to intervene in situations before they become desperate. It is clear that the point of most vulnerability for Edmond related to loss of or potential loss of important relationships. Recognizing the vulnerability of people before they choose violence is very important.

Taking a Stand Against Violence

The first task of the mentor is to take an ethical stand against violence, and also against any system that uses hierarchies of value when assessing human beings. Neither the use of violence for redemptive purposes, nor the hierarchical evaluation of human beings based on their race, gender, or any other immutable characteristic can stand the test of liberated growth. Anyone who attempts to redeem herself or himself from shame by committing an act of violence acts contrary to the Christian gospel. The writer of Hebrews tells us that the life, death, and resurrection of Jesus Christ puts an end to the use of violence as a means of salvation (Hebrews 9). Violence is immoral because it harms rather than fosters the growth of its victims.

Similarly, the determination of value and worth based on gender, race, or social status is in sharp contrast to the hospitality demonstrated by Jesus and his followers in the early church and throughout history. Jesus scandalized his contemporaries by sharing his table with sinners, prostitutes, and tax collectors; and the church he left behind is called to function as one body in which all the members are recognized as of equal value. Ethical systems that assign different values to different people are immoral because they deny the image of God, which all people possess, and cheapen community.

The use of violence to redeem oneself or others from shame, or to redress humiliation at the hands of others, is unacceptable. Violence is the worst possible choice one could make. It is essentially throwing away the lives of those who are involved. No matter the shame or humiliation, no matter the level of devastation associated with the loss of the interpersonal link between persons, resorting to violence or murder destroys both victim and perpetrator and must be rejected.

A Theology for Strategic Intervention

It is my contention that the decision to use violence involves an interpretive process constrained by the possibilities that the perpetrator understands to exist. The range of choices is limited by the individual's experience, by the scenarios presented by the culture, and by the value systems in which we live. Consequently, the mentor must seek to influence the interpretive process that relational refugees use as they contemplate the use of redemptive violence. Influencing the interpretive process begins with a theology.

Violence in the service of self-redemption is destructive to human community and personhood. With Paul, I conclude that revenge belongs to God (Romans 12:9-21). In this passage of scripture, Paul highlights the significance of love and what is good. He says we should practice hospitality and never repay evil with evil. He says we should live peacefully with all people. He writes, "If your enemies are hungry, feed them; if they are thirsty, give them something to drink; for by doing this you will heap burning coals on their heads" (Romans 12:20).

Elsewhere, Paul writes, "No one who believes in [Jesus] will be put to shame" (Romans 10:11). I take this to mean that there is nothing on earth that could cause us enough shame to justify the use of violence in an attempt to redeem ourselves. In fact, Paul points out that Jesus took the road that the world thought was foolish and unwise. Thus, Jesus was about transforming our shame into occasions for ministry. Jesus sought to transform our humiliation and shame into liberated growth for us, as well as for others. The question that confronts us now is how do we get this message across to a world bent on vengeance, on redeeming humiliation with violence, on repaying evil with evil?

Mentors As Public Theologians

My first response is that African American practical theologians and mentors are first and foremost public theologians. Robert Franklin has aptly spelled out the meaning of this term. He writes:

> I believe that all religious leaders or clergy should become public theologians such as Martin Luther King, Jr., Benjamin E. Mays, Marian Wright Edelman and Andrew Young. Public theologians are committed to presenting their understanding of God, ethical principles, and moral values to the larger public for scrutiny, discussion and possible acceptance. In contrast to sectarian theologians who understand that they are speaking for and to the community of believers, public theologians understand themselves to be ambassadors for Christ (2 Corinthians 5:18).[4]

Franklin goes on to say that the public theologian is one who also has a distinctive vision that she or he attempts to bring to bear on the issues faced in a secularized and pluralistic world, with a deep sense of respect for differing belief systems and worldviews. The public theologian stands within a particular faith tradition and must bring the resources of this faith tradition to bear on public issues in ways that the public can grasp and understand. With this in mind, it is important to outline what practical theologians, mentors to relational refugees who are tempted to turn to violence, would do in concrete terms.

Strategic Intervention

The public, practical theologian must first and vigilantly address the many ways in which violence is portrayed as acceptable in the stories, plots, and themes of our culture. We must not only speak about the moral limitations of this type of violence, we must also constantly draw on human examples that demonstrate the shortcomings of turning to its use. While many American movies and moviemakers continue to perpetuate the view that violence is a viable solution to our problems, public theologians must find and promote films such as *Hoodlum* that serve as counterbalances.

Second, we must help people discern that there is a hidden principle of justice at work in life, despite the evil and injustice done in the world. This principle has been a major theme of the spiritual and religious heritage of African Americans. Our proverbs tell us that we never get away with the evil we do. It will always find us out no matter what and no matter how long. It is inevitable. Therefore, there is no real need to take justice into our own hands. There are plenty of examples in the history of the United States of how the vigilante mentality does not serve the ends of liberated growth. Public and practical theologians must continually keep before the public the idea of a hidden justice process that is quietly at work and of the futility of vigilantism.

At the level of role enactment, we must continually reject claims that perpetrators had no other possible courses of action. At the same time, we must expand the repertoire of options that people can recognize and draw upon. Those who feel limited to certain roles based on their race or sex must be encouraged to reject the self-images they are constrained by, even as we also work to dismantle the structures of power that create and maintain these constraints.

Public theologians must also raise the consciousness of their constituencies about issues such as domestic violence. Examples of what it looks like for men and women to live together in mutual and egalitarian relationships need to be upheld. More will be said about male and female relationships in the next chapter.

At the role level, examples of what it means to work through issues without resorting to violence need to be sought and shared in public forums. It is not enough to condemn violence, people must be able to see what peace looks like as well. Thus, our role as practical and public theologians is to comb the world of human experience to find examples of the love of God truly at work. We are long on examples of violence but short on examples of peace. We need to investigate peacemaking in the world with as much vigor as the paparazzi pursue a photograph of a celebrity. Such examples are few and difficult to find. They do exist, however.

At the level of scene and attitude enactment, the task of public and practical theologians is to surround those who have been victimized by evil with loving support and affection as they recover. We are to draw them into the fellowship of God's eschatological community through our love. Our task is to make sure that people have counterexperiences so that the scenes of abuse and oppression are replaced with new, healing ones. We also must make sure that nurturing and supportive people are available for the victims of violence so that they have opportunities to reimagine themselves in new ways, neutralizing the internalized saboteurs who destroy self-esteem. Violence makes victims potential relational refugees. Perhaps this is one of the main reasons people want revenge today.

The question remains, however, how do we deal with people who are the most likely to use violence for redemption? What about young men like Edmond? How do we influence their thought processes? This is a difficult question to answer since those structures that once supported African Americans are slowly deteriorating. The development of strategies to address the needs of the emotionally homeless is a daunting task, but there are signs of hope.

I have been gratified by a grassroots movement taking place among African American men and women that understands that the battle against violence, humiliation, and shame takes place at a very basic level. Men teaching boys how to be men, by example, in the context of intimate, mentoring relationships is the level where the work needs to be done. The same is true for women and girls, and I am pleased that there is a growing movement of mentoring programs for young girls. There is a realization that all of our young people, regardless of gender, lack strong cross-generational bonds through which many of the mimetic lessons are learned. Indeed, the battle against violence must be won and fought at the basic relational level. This is the missing ingredient in our social and political activism. Our activism must include the creation and sustenance of active nurturing relationships, as well as the pursuit of full participation in the social and political structures of the United States.

Conclusion

The leaders of the Civil Rights movement challenged this country "to get at the source of the problem." They meant that structural problems of racism and the response of political action were the venues for bringing about real change. However, this concentration on the social dimensions of the problem resulted in the neglect of the relational and emotional needs of our community. We simply took them for granted.

Today, we have many relational and emotional refugees in the African American community who need to be reincorporated into caring support systems. I am convinced that part of the reason people resort to violence is the absence of emotional relationships where they are considered important. To lose a relationship in today's environment is catastrophic, and some may turn to violence as a protest and a futile attempt at a solution. The true solution is to recognize and help the relational refugees that this post-baby boom generation has produced. The practical public theologian takes seriously the problem of relational refugees, as well as the larger social and cultural problems that are related to them.

CHAPTER THREE

ANIMOSITY IN INTIMATE RELATIONSHIPS AND THE RELATIONAL REFUGEE

Stella had a long history of unsuccessful relationships with men. She was unable to become intimate. At the same time, in her early twenties, she wanted very much to find and get close to the special person who would eventually become her husband.

Stella approached me about counseling after a hostile encounter with a young man who had made inappropriate sexual remarks to her. She was deeply offended by the incident, even after the young man apologized. On the face of it, the incident seemed minor, but she could not let it go. The unfortunate event stirred up feelings that she could no longer ignore.

In counseling, Stella's story unfolded. Her father had initiated an incestuous relationship with her that lasted several years. She kept this relationship a secret for several more years. Every day of secrecy drove her further and further away from her family. She slowly cut herself off from them. Now she felt totally alone in the world and without a home. She had become a relational refugee, although she wanted desperately to reconnect with her family. She felt like a ship abandoned at sea without an anchor.

Our counseling focused on her twin desires; to rejoin her family of origin and to be married. She came to understand that she had to reveal her secret if she expected to connect with her family of origin again. She knew that revealing the secret had the potential to sever those relationships forever, but not revealing it carried the same death sentence.

My role as her counselor was to help her face the incestuous event and the damage it did to her. The more we talked about the

53

details the more courage she developed about confronting her father. Eventually, she confronted her father and revealed the secret to her family.

In the revelation process, something significant happened. Her father, who had, in the meantime, undergone a religious conversion, confirmed the truth of her story and told the family about what he had done. He expressed how deeply sorry he felt for the pain and agony he had caused his daughter and his family. In fact, he called me on the phone to confirm the truth to me, and he vowed to do whatever he could to make sure his daughter was restored to wholeness. After several months, she was able to forgive her father, and she felt better about her relationship with the entire family.

This story raises several important issues and concerns regarding relational refugees. Chief among them is the animosity that exists between males and females. Many couples need help from counselors, pastors, and other mentors to achieve more wholesome and healthy dynamics in intimate relationships.

For Stella, the incestuous relationship nearly destroyed the possibility for a healthy relationship with a man. She brought her feelings of exploitation and anger into every other relationship. She had to work through her own past and confront head-on the cultural norms of male privilege in order to ready herself for the vulnerability of intimacy. She knew firsthand how men can misuse their power to hurt women. She had to gain enough strength of her own to feel safe before she could let a man close to her again.

In this chapter, I analyze the animosity between men and women and the reason it contributes to situations that force people to become relational refugees. I draw on examples from African American literature to help me examine, in more detail, dimensions of this animosity, the reasons for it, and possible solutions to it. My overall goal is to present insights that will help others mentor men and women, from animosity to mutuality, so that they can find community with each other.

Toni Morrison's Insight Into the Animosity Between Men and Women

In several different works, Toni Morrison describes the animosity and conflict between African American men and women. Through her literary pen, her characters struggle together across the lines of gender, sometimes finding healthy ways to relate, sometimes existing in conflict, and sometimes being sent adrift as relational refugees.

In *The Bluest Eye* Morrison traces the animosity between men and women all the way back to the Fall of Adam and Eve. Although she draws her ultimate understanding from the original conflict between men and women, which rests on ancient religious themes, she adds her own lens of race and gender analysis to the descriptions of these problems. In the patriarchal version of the Fall, the point of the story is the introduction of sin into the world by Satan, through his persuasion of Eve to convince Adam to eat the forbidden fruit. Thus, the interpreters have said, women are the source of sin. Morrison offers a new reading.

The Bluest Eye is the tragic story of a family caught in the cross fire of racism and their own stubborn animosity. Cholly, the father, is an unrepentant reprobate who cannot avoid trouble. He is a model relational refugee, unable to find his way out of the misery and harm into which he was born. Abandoned by his biological mother, he was rescued from the garbage heap by an aging aunt, who raised him but also confused his sexual development by forcing him to sleep with her during cold winter nights. His aunt died just as he entered puberty. Soon after her funeral, while engaged in sex with a female peer, Cholly and his partner are discovered by a group of white men who terrorize the couple by making them continue the sex act under their gaze as they shout racial epithets. Just like Adam, Cholly blames his partner for seducing him, rather than blaming the men for terrorizing him. Later, he searches out his father but on finding him is summarily rejected. At the climax of the story, Cholly rapes his own daughter, Pecola.

Mrs. Breedlove is Cholly's wife and Pecola's mother. She prides herself on the striking contrast between her character and Cholly's. She needs his failures to make her own uprightness glow all the brighter by comparison. She suffers his waywardness rather than trying to help him change because it keeps their dynamics stable, if not healthy. Morrison writes: "Mrs. Breedlove considered herself an upright and Christian woman, burdened with a no-count man, whom God wanted her to punish."[1] Mrs. Breedlove's superior status is also reinforced because she works for important white people. As a servant of these people, Mrs. Breedlove did not have to wait in line to make purchases or accept inferior grades of food. On her own she would have no special status but as an employee of the power she gains power herself.

Apparently, Mrs. Breedlove and Cholly derived some twisted purpose for their existence from this insane daily dance of animosity. It was almost as if they feared stopping the waltz of enmity, thinking that life would have no meaning if they resolved their conflict. They had no vision of what their marriage could be if they were not dancers in this waltz of tragic marital madness. Over and over again, they acted out the warped dynamics foretold in the story of the Fall. But, in this telling, it is clear that neither woman nor man was solely responsible, rather they participated in a complementary destructive dance, where one partner played the superior role and the other the inferior role. In this dance, they cemented themselves in their alienated status and reinforced, rather than healed, the traumas that had led to their conflicts, their entrapment as relational refugees.

Relational Refugees Within the Marriage Covenant

Morrison's novel reveals that relational refugees can exist even within relationships. Men and women in a marriage can be in such conflict that they hold each other at a distance and are essentially disconnected. All relationships require hard work, a commitment to work out issues that divide and separate. Intimacy is slowly gained through effort, not conferred by a license or even a ceremony of solemn vows. Some participants are simply unable or unwilling to undertake this work. Among spouses not fully present to their partners are those we call relational refugees.

Specific scenes in the novel provide helpful insight about the process people follow as they become relational refugees. *The Bluest Eye* is full of negative scenes. Even positive situations degrade into negative scenarios. Morrison's message seems to be that nothing can be trusted. In such a nihilistic situation, relational refugees flourish. Witnessing the tragedy that comes from these negative relationships, the reader concludes that there is no substitute for loving and caring relationships, that all people need relationships with people of the same sex, with people of the opposite sex, and with people of different generations.

The implication for mentoring is clear. Mentors need to help their charges create the kind of community where nurturing relationships are cultivated. In the context of a troubled marriage, or any other type of relationship between a man and a woman, mentors must be aware that very often one or both partners have a past that makes it difficult for them to participate fully in the relationship. The relational refugee will not find it comfortable to be identified as the one who is unable or unwilling to relate to her or his partner in healthy ways, and will find it even harder to change those patterns. The mentor must invite the relational refugee into new ways of being that honor the level of resistance she or he might have.

Strategic Intervention

Mentoring involves helping the relational refugee feel at home in the world emotionally, spiritually, relationally, and cognitively. The first strategic activity of mentors should be what I call "faithing." From the shadow that the Fall has cast over male and female relationships, it appears that the possibilities of us living in caring, supportive, nurturing, and egalitarian relationships are few indeed. From the light of Christ, however, a different view of possibilities occurs. From the perspective of faith, the mentor can discern, in the midst of a broken relationship, God's active presence. From the perspective of faith, the couple can begin to see that God is at work freeing them from their destructive dynamics, and, in fact, liberating all bonds of intimacy between males and females from the curse of the Fall. The mentor can offer plots and scenes from the tradition of faith that can serve as resources for the couple that wants to move from conflict to camaraderie.

In fact, in many marital and family situations, it is often the mentor's faith that sustains couples and families until they find their own hope. Engaging in the process of pastoral counseling and helping people explore their lives, with the confidence that things can be different, often is enough to bring hope. Sometimes families populated by relational refugees enter counseling sessions depressed and demoralized. They cannot see past the frustration and hopelessness of the present dynamics. However, simply engaging in the process of analysis can present to them new possibilities, rays of hope.

A skilled mentor can point to those hidden, yet discernible, instances of God's presence within even the most difficult circumstances. In Alice Walker's *The Color Purple,* Nettie provides her sister Celie with hope during Celie's despair over her unhealthy marriage. Nettie writes from Africa where she serves as an assistant to missionaries who, unbeknownst to Celie, have adopted Celie's children, children conceived when their stepfather raped Celie repeatedly over a number of years. Her letter is an example for mentors of how to faith a relational refugee. Nettie writes:

> Oh, Celie, there are colored people in the world who want us to know! Want us to grow and see the light! They are not all mean like Pa and Albert, or beaten down like ma was. Corrine and Samuel have a wonderful marriage. Their only sorrow in the beginning was that they could not have children. And then, they say, "God" sent them Olivia and Adam.[2]

Thus, Samuel and Corrine are examples of recipients of God's favor during their own grief over being childless. Their good fortune gives hope to Nettie and Celie. They are, as well, the saviors of Celie's children who were thought to be lost. The children that filled the void in their lives turn out to be Celie's children, a coincidence that Nettie experiences as a miracle.

Like Pharaoh's daughter who found baby Moses in the bulrushes and brought him out of the water and into the palace, and who had his own mother serve as wetnurse, Samuel and Corrine adopt Olivia and Adam when Celie's stepfather takes them away. When Nettie runs away before also becoming a victim of her stepfather's lust, Samuel and Corrine notice her resemblance to the children and hire her to help care for them. Samuel and Corrine are a human couple with the foibles we all share but they are able to live faithfully with each other because of their spiritual grounding. In turn, God is able to use them to turn a story of grief and loss into a story of life and hope.

After searching out evidence of God's care within the relationship, the mentor or counselor can engage in a second stage of strategic intervention which I call "narrative reliance." Narrative reliance is an awareness that God's plans often operate like narrative plots. That is, they unfold slowly rather than all at once, with many twists and turns, rather than simply. Faith is the trust that God's promises, however obscure they may seem as the plot unfolds, are sure. Once the mentor helps the couple identify God's presence in the history of their life together, she or he must help them trust God to bring them to the promised end of wholeness. Relational refugees need to learn to live in hope rather than fear, to rely on the unfolding narrative of God's love for them.

The mentor helps people to attend to God's presence in their lives despite the trouble that brought them to seek help. Nettie was able to see God at work in the lives of the African American missionaries for whom she worked. She had the ability to identify the miracle that brought her broken family back together. Not every miracle is obvious to us, and so we need people who can discern the miracles that lie below the surface of our lives and point them out to us.

After faithing and encouraging narrative reliance, the mentor must inculcate critical realism in the couple. While learning to live in an intimate relationship means opening oneself to change and to articulating what one needs and expects from the other person, there are limits to what one can ask of that person. So we must be both critical, of ourselves and of the other individual, and realistic about the limits of the capacity to change. The mentor needs to help the couple identify and accept those aspects of the relationship that they cannot change, even as they work diligently to change those aspects of the relationships that they can improve.

Mentors must not always assume that an easy answer exists to the couple's problems. Instead, he or she must provide a relational context for working through problems. When I serve as a mentor, I attempt to help people overcome romantic notions and triumphal expectations about my ability to improve their predicament. Easy answers only encourage frustration because they do not transform the essential dynamics of the relationship and therefore only put off conflict rather than resolve it. My strategy is to engage the couple in a process of growth. I much prefer to have the couple commit to the counseling process than to the fact of their commitment. They need to expect both progress and setbacks. With those who are familiar with biblical metaphors, I suggest that they cultivate a wilderness orientation to life rather than a promised land perspective. A wilderness orientation keeps the end goal in mind but suggests that the path toward the promised land is a long and circuitous one. For the Hebrew slaves newly freed from Egypt, the journey to the land of milk and honey took forty years and was filled with many moments of backsliding and disorientation. The experience of reaching the promised land of marital bliss is not so different.

Healthy relationships require even more than an attitude of critical realism, however. The couple must not only look inward at their own dynamics, but also out to the world around them, toward which they direct themselves through their vocational commitment. Samuel and Corrine again serve as models. They lived as a loving couple but also found something beyond themselves to which they were committed. They both found their calling as missionaries. After Corrine died, Samuel and Nettie married, and they continued the missionary work. A couple's relationship is strengthened, not weakened, by a shared vocation, or by mutual support of the different vocations of each spouse. The mentor must remind those with whom she or he works that working together to serve others is a critical part of forming a loving relationship. Marriages are not only for the good of the couple but also for the good of the community in which it is constituted.

Again, I emphasize that mentoring involves not only telling people how they should live and what dynamics they should cultivate, but also modeling these behaviors. Counselors and pastors should preach and teach about healthy ways of relating, but must also provide examples of these ways.[3] We must form communities filled with people who can demonstrate what it means to live together as men and women of faith—trustworthy, compassionate, and strong. All of our church programs, our preaching, counseling, Christian education, and administrative planning should communicate that we take people's relationships seriously. We need to encourage our people to form and strengthen relationships with those of the same age and with those of different age groups, with those of the same gender and those of the opposite sex. Human beings are social creatures and there is no more important aspect of our ministry than the nurturing of whole and wholesome relationships among the members of our communities.

The relationship between a man and a woman, the marital bond, is the core relationship within all others. For without the couple there is no family and without the family there is no church. Furthermore, marriage in our tradition, is understood to communicate the love of God for the church. The love between a husband and wife shows us in flesh and blood how God loves God's people. But, as we know and have seen, these relationships are also particularly difficult to sustain in healthy ways. In contrast to God's perfect and everlasting love, the love between a man and woman is fragile, often painful, and sometimes hurtful. But God works through us as we use fragile earthen vessels. In our relationships, even in the moments of conflict, God is present, working with us for our own good. We are not doomed to reenact the brokenness of the Fall. We have limits from which we work, but our reflection on problems, in light of our faith and practice, can help us exercise the actual freedom that we have to let go of patterns of fear and fall into life sustaining intimacy.

CHAPTER FOUR

ADOLESCENCE AND
THE RELATIONAL
REFUGEE

Human identity is formed in a matrix of relationships. We discover ourselves in and through our encounters with others. Our sense of "me" is dependent on the existence of a "you." We can only see our own eyes in the reflection of another's. Human identity is also not a possession but a process. We come to discover ourselves more fully throughout our lifetimes. Adolescence, a stage betwixt and between, involves substantial physical and emotional changes. Raging hormones affect adolescents' moods as well as bodies. The drive to be independent is matched only by the great emotional neediness of the period. It is a time when many are at risk of becoming relational refugees.

Young men and women attempt to discover themselves but are dependent on how others treat them in this process. Some are strong enough to resist experiences of harm or neglect but others are not. Those at risk of becoming relational refugees are those who believe that they are worthless and that they must pretend to be someone else in order to be considered valuable. Adolescents sort through a jumble of messages, both internal and external, as they arrive at some sort of self-understanding. Parents, the church, peers, and teachers all send cues to young people suggesting what they should believe and who they should be. Many young people come to believe that what they think is really of no great consequence. Some get the idea that to be of significance, they have to be someone other than themselves. They strive for affirmation by fitting themselves into someone else's prescribed set of expectations that are often alien to who they truly are. Those who insist on defining themselves by the standards of others will become relational refugees.

In this chapter I explore black adolescent identity formation, particularly, the importance of receiving confirmation of one's own sense of self for healthy identity development, from one's environment and from significant others. Adolescents especially need consistent affirmation by others who provide positive plots, roles, scenes, and attitudes on which the young persons can draw for their behavioral choices and worldview.

The eminent developmental psychologist Erik Erikson has pointed out that healthy self-identity is very difficult for young African Americans to develop in a society that communicates only negative attitudes toward African Americans.[1] Toni Morrison explores these same issues in her novel *The Bluest Eye*. In the previous chapter, I discussed the relationship between Cholly and Mrs. Breedlove from this same narrative. Here, I look at the experience of their daughter, Pecola, a young black woman growing up in the United States during the pre–Civil Rights era of the 1940s. Pecola serves as a model for my reflections on mentoring African American young people through the rough terrain of adolescence in a land of racism.

The Bluest Eye

This book is Toni Morrison's account of a young African American girl, who is growing up in a family, a community, and a world in which black means ugly. The book depicts, in graphic detail, the process through which Pecola learns to hate and despise what she sees in the mirror. Hating the way one looks, one's physical appearance and one's color, has to be carefully taught, and Morrison takes the time to narrate the learning of self-hatred.

Pecola comes to believe that she would be acceptable to herself and others if she had blue eyes. The world values blue eyes. They are often a symbol of the superiority of whiteness. Pecola's fixation with acquiring blue eyes contributes to her demise. She undergoes a psychotic break with reality. Everyone around her confirms that she is ugly rather than help her see that beauty is only skin deep. Abandoned by those who should provide her with support, Pecola becomes a relational refugee.

Self-Hatred Is Caught Like a Disease

Pecola's sense of self-worth is attacked on two major fronts: the racist, classist, and sexist standards of beauty of the larger society, and the stubborn convictions of her own dysfunctional family. This combined attack proved irresistible, especially because she had so few allies, so few resources to preserve her self-esteem.

Pecola succumbs to the standards of her culture, just as many of us do, because the messages are so powerful, constant, and inescapable. Morrison reminds so many of her readers of how we come to hate ourselves:

> Adults, older girls, shops, magazines, newspapers, window signs—all the world had agreed that a blue-eyed, yellow-haired, pink-skinned doll was what every girl child treasured. "Here," they said, "this is beautiful, and if you are on this day 'worthy' you may have it."[2]

These values of the wider culture sank deeply and unimpeded into Pecola's psyche.

Pecola could not resist the many voices that told her that she was ugly and that blond haired, blue-eyed dolls were pretty. However, the standards of beauty were not the sole cause of Pecola's self-hatred. Pecola did not just think that she was not beautiful, she was convinced that she was ugly. This sense of ugliness was profound and had roots not outside in the world, but deep within her own home.

Morrison helps us to see that learning ugliness can be a part of a family legacy, carefully passed on from one generation to the next. Morrison describes Pecola's heritage:

> The Breedloves did not live in a storefront because they were having temporary difficulty adjusting to the cutbacks at the plant. They lived there because they were poor and black, and they stayed there because they believed they were ugly. Although their poverty was traditional and stultifying, it was not unique. But their ugliness was unique. No one could have convinced them that they were not relentlessly and aggressively ugly. Except for the father, Cholly, whose ugliness (the result of despair, dissipation, and violence directed toward petty things and weak people) was behavior, the rest of the family—Mrs. Breedlove, Sammy Breedlove, and Pecola

Breedlove—wore their ugliness, put it on, so to speak, although it did not belong to them.[3]

In another passage, Morrison continues, "You looked at them and wondered why they were so ugly; you looked closely and could not find the source. Then you realized that it came from conviction, their conviction."[4] The family defined itself by the standards of the world, standards that defined them as hopelessly inferior. They internalized the wider cultural attitude, then passed it on to their children, as if it were the simple truth. As we saw in the previous chapter, Cholly and Mrs. Breedlove are trapped in an endless maze of destructive relational patterns. Their relationship as husband and wife is a breeding ground for self-hatred. They agree not to kill each other physically, settling instead for dying a slow emotional and spiritual death by denying daily each other's value and worth.

Pecola is a victim of her parents' dysfunction over and over again. Her father commits the ultimate act of emotional destruction by raping her. Her mother emotionally abandons her to serve her white employers. In scene after scene, Pecola's legacy of self-hatred was reinforced. Without alternatives, she internalizes the attitudes of those around her. At every level, her self-esteem is eroded. In this sick relational environment, Pecola could hardly avoid becoming a relational refugee.

At one point in the novel, Morrison has Pecola compare herself to a dandelion.[5] Pecola wonders why people do not like dandelions. She notes that people use dandelions to make soups and wine and yet work hard to keep them out of their gardens and yards. Pecola feels like a dandelion, available to be used but kept out of sight, exploited yet disdained.

Pecola might have escaped her tragic fate if she had some support, some person or persons who could confirm her beauty and self-worth. Pecola is taken in by a family that includes the narrator, a girl who speaks in Morrison's voice, who has rejected the standards of beauty that her culture values, who thinks blonde haired, blue-eyed dolls are ugly. This character, Morrison, and her sister, Frieda, are portrayed as Pecola's only friends, but their friendship with her is not enough to kill the weeds of self-hatred planted in her life. Though Frieda and Morrison adored Pecola, the crack in the dam of her self-esteem continues to widen.

Mentoring

Pecola is an adolescent girl. Morrison makes clear that black women suffer the violence of sexism, as well as racism. To form a healthy self-identity, black girls contend against these interlocking structures of oppression. As womanist scholars have made clear, African American women survive and thrive despite multiple levels of persecution.[6] African American adolescent girls need support to fight the attacks on their self-esteem on these various levels. Pecola had to search for an alternative to the blue-eyed standards of beauty but also needed to heal from the betrayal of trust by her parents, especially from her father's sexual violence.

The process of identity formation for young black men is no less difficult than that of young black women. Black men contend with racial oppression but have access to sexist privilege, nonetheless, suffering is not a matter of comparison by simple addition. The long traditions of Western racism makes the search for self-esteem difficult for all those not born with white skin.[7] I highlight the female example here to affirm the multiple attacks on their self-worth but I proceed in my discussion of pastoral responses, concentrating primarily on the obstacles placed before young people by racism.

Mentors who become involved in supporting young people in their struggle to find and sustain a healthy self-identity must begin by affirming the irrevocable value of all people that is foundational to our spiritual traditions. Ultimately, one's true value comes from one's relationship with God. The world around you may dismiss you as inferior. Your family may hurt rather than support you. You may not believe you are worth much. But, our traditions say, "you are a child of God." Thus, no one, not the abandoned, raped, dark-skinned, "ugly" girl, nor any other human being, is an orphan. We belong to the family of God. This must be the starting point for anyone who hopes to rescue adolescent relational refugees.

As a consequence, the mentor might continue, we must treat others as equals for they too are God's children. To harm, shame, or neglect another member of the family of God is a sin. Moreover, to accept images abroad in the wider society that denigrate the self is a form of idolatry, because it obscures God's validation. African Americans have proved skillful at revaluing the self. Devalued by the society in which we live, we look to God for affirmation. Enslaved, we found in God freedom promised and fulfilled. We might have been forced to live in bondage, but we did not regard ourselves as slaves.

For many African Americans, the black church, the black family, and the black institutions of higher education have been the countercultural training ground where the message of worth and value could be heard and internalized. These sanctuaries of affirmation in a culture of discrimination provided a place to contend with the demons of racism. Yet, self-hatred rooted in the internalization of racist and sexist ideologies could not be completely eradicated by these institutions. Not only do African Americans have to move across the thresholds of these sanctuaries and out into a hostile culture at various times, the ideologies of the larger world permeate these supposedly safe havens, as well. The internalization of racism and sexism is ethically and morally unacceptable. The question, then, is how do we strategically intervene in the process of African American adolescent personality development to support young people in their journeys toward self-acceptance and liberated growth?

Strategic Intervention

In *Paradise,* a more recent example of Morrison's work, she tells the story of an African American town in Oklahoma after the Civil Rights revolution of the 1960s. The scars from this community's long battle for freedom from oppression and injustice are so deep that there is no energy left with which to nurture the emerging personalities of the town's youth. Morrison narrates the failure of the first post–Civil Rights generation of parents and grandparents to support the growth and development of their children.

Morrison simply tells the tale of these families. She does not analyze the reasons for the inadequate parenting that occurred. However, some possibilities exist in my mind. First, post–Civil Rights parents, like the children of Israel following the Exodus from bondage in Egypt, may simply have concluded that the battle of oppression was over, that children growing up after the hard-won passage of Civil Rights laws did not need as much support at home. Perhaps, we assumed that the end of segregation ended as well the assault on black self-esteem so that our young people would just fall automatically into line. Second, the first post–Civil Rights generation shifted their energies from the struggle for equality to pursuing careers and material wealth in the newly accessible arenas of the mainstream corporate world. Our well-intentioned efforts to escape poverty or otherwise offer our children a better start than we had may have resulted in a neglect of other needs. We simply may have become too busy to raise our own children.

Archie Smith has noted that in this period many African Americans made a drastic shift in strategy. If in the Civil Rights era we had worked for the overthrow of the systems of inequality, afterwards we sought to become middle class, to join and benefit from capitalist economic structures. For Smith, the economic system itself functions to maintain rather than alleviate inequality. He makes the further claim that entering into market-based relationships spiritually impoverishes the participants. For black people, the destruction of supportive networks in favor of consumerist models of community is especially damaging.[8] In our effort to get our piece of the American pie, we have forgotten our responsibility to nurture the next generation. We have been deceived into thinking that all was well. Our children's self-esteem is therefore very much at risk. God's liberation is never a call to join the ranks of the oppressors or to benefit from their spoils. Rather, our liberation is a call to service and social transformation. "We have come over a way that with tears has been watered."[9]

The African American faith community must reclaim its prominence in nurturing the next generation of leaders. The church has been the training ground for most of the great leaders in our history. But today, for the first time, African American young people can conceive of the possibility of not being members of the faith community. Whereas we must accept the pluralism of the current age and the suspicion of all institutions, including religious ones, that now pervades our society, we must all reassert the power of the church in the continuing struggle for equality and justice, for social and personal transformation.

In the next few pages, I offer some reflections on how parents and community leaders, who indeed accept their vocation to raise the next generation, can encourage the healthy development of young people today. The first point to recognize is that personal transformation and social transformation are intricately linked. Smith, drawing on the work of Vincent Harding, outlines the following process of growth that bridges the two spheres. First an individual must tap or rediscover a sense of meaning. This results in a discovery of personal agency. When accompanied by the development of a critical perspective on the status quo, the individual is ready to take some action for change. Commitment to sustain such action is based in the discovery of a vocation of service. In this way, the effort to humanize the world is linked to personal renewal.[10]

Thirty years after the Kerner Commission Report on the state of the various racial/ethnic groups in the United States, there was a follow-up study.[11] The conclusions of this report include observations that America's neighborhoods and schools are resegregating and the number of children who live in poverty has increased 20 percent since the 1980s. Although the economic and social situation of African Americans, as a group, has improved during this period, things have become worse for many individual families. For instance, black youths remain disproportionately likely to be unemployed or imprisoned. On a more personal level, I observe this generation of parents has too often abdicated the responsibility of raising its offspring so that grandparents must fill the gap. At this time, it is critical that adults reclaim their role as mentors for young people, especially youth at risk.

The Ecumenical Families Alive Project is an important example of programs that address the needs of young people. Funded by the Robert Wood Johnson Foundation and staffed by Anne Streaty Wimberly, other members of the Interdenominational Theological Center faculty, and community leaders, the program provides assistance to grandparents raising grandchildren and to other families with troubled youth. Through visits, telephone hot lines, support groups, referrals, and advocacy, the volunteers support the primary caregivers and serve as role models for the youth.

Adolescents need a variety of resources to help them grow and flourish. They need stories of heroes and heroines to inspire them. They need traditions that testify to God's presence in the struggle to become a mature human being who lives responsibly in community. They need mentors who provide listening ears and other types of support. They need hope that the constraints on their lives are not the deepest reality, that the limitations of racism, for instance, do not have the last word on their future.

For stories, let us follow Archie Smith's suggestions that we engage in "reflexivity," in a reexamination of the past for valuable lessons which can stimulate imagination for new possibilities and new outcomes.[12] Looking back allows us to tap the deep spiritual resources that ignited the Civil Rights movements and other black liberation movements and which still sustain the black family and extended family. Looking back we encounter the loving and transforming God of history who acts for justice and peace still. Looking back we join in a hermeneutics of engagement, an identification of God's active presence in the past, that fuels our movement with God into the future.

The story of Mary McLeod Bethune is one story that I find empowering. I recommend it to those who are engaged in ministries with young people. My father went to Bethune Cookman College, which she helped found, and often told me of her and how she had inspired his own ministry. Bethune was born in 1875. Her mother worked as a domestic. When Mary was little she accompanied her mother to the house of the white family for whom she worked. One day Mary wandered about the neighborhood and came upon two little girls who were playing in their playhouse. The playhouse seemed larger and nicer than the shack that was Mary's home, but nonetheless she ventured in and began to play. The white girls gave Mary their dolls to care for. They were just imitating the realities of their world in which black women cared for white children, but the implication that Mary could play with them only if she took a subservient role was clear. Later, Mary spotted a book in the playhouse and attempted to read. Her playmates scolded her, reminding her that black children were not supposed to learn to read. They put her out of the house as well.

Bethune told this story often, noting how her first experience of white racism was also her first recognition of her desire to learn to read. Her powerful connection to books and learning stems from what on the surface was a negative experience. Her ability to reinterpret her encounter with the white girls stems from her positive self-image that was cultivated among a supportive family and community.

Bethune was not known for her external beauty. She found the necessary spiritual resources from God, her family, and community to recognize her internal beauty instead. Her firm belief in her own worth gave her the confidence and courage to help others, not the least through the establishment of her school. Bethune's story highlights the significance of supportive networks in the healthy development of black youth.

Young people need adults who can teach, through precept and example, proactive responses that our youth can use when they are devalued. We must show them how to stop the erosion of their self-esteem from relationships or experiences that communicate any sense of inferiority. We must help them speak up and speak out when they are devalued. We must help them to assert themselves respectfully and appropriately so that they do not put themselves or others at risk in a confrontation with authority.

Parents are the most important role models for adolescents. But parents are also the primary authorities against which adolescents must rebel as they come to accept and grow into their own authority. As parents, we must be both supportive and accepting. Our children face many obstacles as they grow into adulthood. We must affirm their aspirations and be available to them when they need support. But we must also allow them to define themselves, avoiding the extremes of being overcontrolling on the one hand and abdicating our responsibility on the other. We need to be aware that parenting youth is a process that necessarily involves tension. There is no easy way around the problems of adolescent identity formation. There is also no blueprint or road map. Our adolescent children need to have the assurance that we will always be there for them, that we respect them and the choices they are learning to make, even as we maintain enough limits to keep them safe, and that they can trust us as role models on which to build their own lives. These things will provide a secure home from which they can fly on their own.

Adolescents, especially those who belong to so-called minority communities, need a sense of hope that they can make their biggest dreams come true. Despite all the negative reports about black adolescent unemployment and the incarceration of our black youth, there is some good news as well. Where conformity to the standards of the majority culture used to be a prerequisite for success in the job market, the increasing diversity of our nation and the globalization of the economy means that young people who are skilled in crossing boundaries of culture are now considered assets. The owner of the Carolina Panthers, Jerry Richardson, predicts that the global economy will require a racially diverse workforce in the future. Those who can work together with people of different races and cultures are becoming highly sought after. In Mutare, Zimbabwe, where I wrote this book, I met hopeful black and white youth who have learned to work together for a common, bright future.

Whereas a bright future beckons, the process of identity formation has become no easier for adolescents today. Whether a relational refugee, like Pecola, or a girl blessed with a supportive family despite the racist and sexist culture that surrounded her, like Mary McLeod Bethune, our children all must fight against the demons of self-doubt and shame as they take their places beside us in the making of a better world. As their mentors, parents, and pastors, we must offer them our love and support, modeling for them wholesome and responsible ways of living. They require much of us, but this is our role and we have stories, role models, and each other to rely on as resources for our work with them. We all need to create or strengthen networks of mutually sustaining relationships in which our young people can thrive. Adolescents can so easily be lost. Without close-knit families, school communities, neighborhoods, and churches, they will be spiritually and emotionally impoverished. We were not liberated to become middle class, to accumulate wealth, or to fulfill our own selfish desires. We were liberated to participate in God's transformation of the world, and each of us has a particular calling to fulfill in this regard.

CHAPTER FIVE

POVERTY, PROSPERITY, AND THE RELATIONAL REFUGEE

Lorraine Hansberry's play *A Raisin in the Sun* confronts its audience with the tension between community values and economic opportunity.[1] As I discussed in the previous chapter, the Civil Rights laws gave African Americans access to greater economic opportunity. Many have taken advantage of the legal protections from job and housing discrimination to pursue the American dream of prosperity. At the same time, this pursuit has undermined some of the basic values and commitments that African Americans have historically cultivated. For me, the play raises a fundamental question: At what price should the American dream of economic prosperity be bought?

I certainly understand that everyone must make a living. And I know of no alternative to the capitalist system that could sustain me, or others, materially. But I am concerned that we recognize the discontinuities between our economic behavior and the values of our heritage and do what we can to foster the latter even if it means curtailing the former. African Americans must make a living and at the same time resist the consumerist values of the market culture. It is my firm conviction that wholesale adoption of the values of market capitalism separates us into autonomous consumers who compete with each other to collect and devour products and services. The market disconnects us from each other and encourages us to act selfishly. It fosters a sense of rootlessness in us. It loosens our hold on the meaning of life. The market rewards homeless minds, relational refugees.

A Raisin in the Sun tells the story of an African American family who lives on the south side of Chicago. Three generations share a crowded apartment. They all dream of owning their own home where each family member has her or his own room, where children have a place to play, and where Moma, the matriarch, can have a garden. As the play opens the family awaits impatiently $10,000 of life insurance money. The money is coming because Big Walter, the patriarch, has died.

They all want a better place to live, but there are several other individual dreams as well. Moma and Big Walter have two children, Walter Lee and Berneatha. Walter Lee wants to use some of the money to start a business. Berneatha wants some of the money to be set aside for her to go to medical school. Walter Lee's wife, Ruth, and their son, Travis, also live in the apartment. Ruth agrees with Moma that a house is the priority. Travis just wants everyone to be happy. When the money comes, Moma puts $3,500 down on a house in the white suburbs, and gives the rest of the money to Walter Lee. He promises to save some for Berneatha's education and to invest the rest, but instead invests the entire $6,500. Unfortunately, Walter Lee's partner turns out to be a con man and Walter Lee loses everything.

Walter Lee's dreams are dashed before they even take shape, and because of his selfishness, so are the dreams of his sister. Walter Lee experiences a clash of values, economic and material on one hand, spiritual and relational on the other hand. In the end, he chooses to embrace his family, finding a new sense of self-worth not dependent on the amount of money or things he has accumulated.

Hansberry's play is about a family that seems to gain the entire world but lose its soul. It is also a story about the possibility of finding hope again when dreams are stolen. Hansberry shows her audience how meaning can be found in the midst of disappointment and suffering. She explodes the false myth that money can solve all human problems.

The play also stresses the importance of maintaining relationships across generations and the value of multigenerational narratives of racial pride. It presents an important response to the yearnings of relational refugees in that it shows that it is possible for a household of three generations to work together and maintain harmonious relationships despite setbacks and betrayals.

Practical theological reflection on this play focuses on the ten-

sion between the pursuit of economic prosperity and the maintenance of a family's values. My intention is to provide insight about
the ways African Americans can participate fully in the American
dream and, at the same time, sustain their religious and cultural
heritage.

A Clash of Cultures

None of the characters in Hansberry's play are relational
refugees. Despite all of the conflict over the money, the family
maintains itself and no one is lost, no one walks away; the characters remain in relationship. The play concerns the temptation to
disconnect oneself from one's family in order to fulfill one's own
dreams.

Walter Lee and Berneatha are most at risk for becoming relational refugees. Walter Lee is at risk because of his greed and his
dependence on money for a sense of his own value. Berneatha
rebels against the traditions that sustain her mother, most significantly, she asserts that she does not need Christian faith. Neither of
these two follow through on their tendencies toward refugee status, but their choices reveal the strength of such temptations and
show ways that temptations can be resisted.

Walter Lee is not easy to get along with. He thinks of himself
first. He asserts his primacy as "man of the house" and expects the
women in his life to sacrifice their dreams for his. He is devoted to
his son but only in terms of being a provider for Travis's material
needs and wants. His poverty threatens his sense of himself as a
father. He believes money will prop up his fragile self-esteem. As
the date the check is due to arrive nears, Walter Lee becomes
pleasant to be around. His motto is "I got a dream." The money is,
for him, the path toward fulfillment of this dream. Its approach
makes him happy, but also puts him at risk for the scam that pulls
the rug out from under him.

Moma, representative of the rich family legacy of racial pride,
saves Walter Lee from his own foolishness. She, along with the now
deceased Big Walter, were concerned not only with material well-
being but emotional and spiritual well-being also. Moma tries to
remind her children that Big Walter left them much more than

$10,000. He left them a heritage, an identity, a model of one who, despite poverty, found self-acceptance and lived with pride. When Walter Lee loses the majority of their money, Moma does not attack him. The family is nearly defeated but she allows him a chance at redemption. Walter Lee is offered money by a white homeowner who is willing to pay him if he will agree not to move his family to a predominantly white neighborhood. Moma lets him decide what to do. He is torn between the values of the culture and the values of his family. This time he chooses to let the money go and choose a better life for his family, a life that also contributes to the welfare of his entire community. Moma is a model parent and mentor here. She provides guidance for Walter Lee but then allows him to learn from his mistakes and have the power to choose again.

Moma serves as a model parent and mentor in relation to Berneatha as well. In contrast to her brother, Berneatha rejected the values of the dominant culture and looked to Africa for her identity. She left the church and other central aspects of African American life because she felt they were too closely connected to the culture of the oppressors. By embracing African traditions, she asserted her individual identity and resisted the pressure to assimilate. Moma accepted her daughter's need to take a different path but modeled a middle way. Moma both preserved her racial dignity and participated fully in the wider culture.

Walter Lee's and Berneatha's decisions represent the two poles of the many choices facing African Americans as they find a way to live in a racist culture. Walter Lee, for a variety of reasons having to do with his sense of himself as a man, a father, and a poor black, struggled mightily to choose between get-rich-quick schemes and the rich legacy of values of his family. His temptation was to assimilate and accept the values of the market over the good of his family. Berneatha sought to express herself, to leave behind the trappings of America for her personal interpretation of African culture. Her temptation was to reject assimilation in a way that reflected modern individualism. Both were tempted to abandon their heritage for different reasons and in opposite directions. Moma's enduring values bridged the two spheres of realities.

Moma embraced what Andrew Billingsley would call bicultural or double consciousness. Bicultural consciousness is the ability to be both black and American simultaneously.[2] Full assimilation into wider society is not ideal for African American families, according to Billingsley. Rather, the African American genius has been the ability to maintain enduring, distinct, cultural kinship patterns, religious values, and a strong work ethic while participating in the socioeconomic structures of the wider culture. This stubborn strength to hold a self together when it is pulled in two directions has engendered whatever success African Americans have achieved. Moma and Big Walter embodied these values, this alternative to assimilation and individualism.

Values of the Religious and Social Legacy

One key value of the African American faith tradition is the ability to find hope and meaning in the midst of tragedy and difficulty. This has been a mainstay of our tradition.[3] African American faith traditions, like the biblical texts on which they are based, include many stories of people of faith enduring tough times, wilderness wanderings. And, as in the Bible, the testimonies, the stories of martyrs and saints, tell us over and over again that God's active presence was encountered on those stony roads. In situations of poverty, God sustains until the rains come or the check clears. In situations of shattered, deferred, or exploding dreams, God appears and a word of hope is heard one more time.

Hansberry wrote *A Raisin in the Sun* when the Civil Rights revolution was in full swing. It was a time of great hope and anticipation that new and better economic horizons were dawning. The play acknowledges how limited actual opportunities were, however. The housing discrimination patterns were breaking down, and African Americans could buy homes in white neighborhoods. Whereas white racism still haunted these sales, they could not stop them. In the case of the Younger family, other obstacles existed. It was Walter Lee's behavior that threatened the family's hopes and dreams. He squandered their money on a get-rich-quick scam. The play shows that threats to economic security exist within the African American community, as well as from outside it. African American leaders have debated the value of self-help in reversing the economic situation of the community. Poor people must learn by example and precept about economic structures and the ways in which they can organize and discipline themselves to contribute to the well-being of the entire community.

The play stresses the importance of grounding masculine identity not in the exploitative values of the marketplace, but in a commitment to the needs of the next generation. Moma offers Big Walter as a example for Walter Lee to emulate. Big Walter's manhood rested in his contribution to a five-generation-long legacy of racial pride and to the growth and development of the next generation. It was difficult for Walter Lee to accept his father's model of masculinity, but he came to see its strength and authenticity.

The play also offers insight into values of parenting, of helping a son become a man and helping a daughter learn to love. I have already mentioned Moma's skill in enabling Walter Lee to redeem himself when he was offered money to not move into the white neighborhood. In another scene, after Walter Lee lost the $6,500, Berneatha wanted to disown him. In response, Moma preached a sermon to Berneatha about love. She asked her daughter when did she think it was appropriate to love? Then she answered her own question: "It's when he's at his lowest and can't believe in hisself 'cause the world done whipped him so!"[4] Thus, Moma gave her daughter the secret to facilitating manhood, to love men regardless, but especially when they are down. Such love is not a weak love that does not challenge a man to stand up when he falls. Such love abides and takes the risk of offering the man another opportunity to try. Withdrawing love from persons when they are at their lowest point can seal their self-destruction. Moma, however, never withdrew her love from Walter Lee, and he was able to internalize it and use it for his own growth, as well as for the growth of others.

In the end, family members were able to embrace Moma's double consciousness, able to move toward a future of full participation in American society, without losing their footing in their own heritage. The blind embrace of the values of the marketplace leads ultimately to the destruction of families. Incorporating one's commitment to self, family, community, and village into one's attitude toward money and work keeps one in balance. This, at least, is my interpretation of Hansberry's lesson for how we as African Americans are supposed to relate to the market economy in the latter part of the twentieth century and into the twenty-first century.

Strategic Intervention

Postindustrial capitalism strains human relationships on many levels. Competitive models appear to encourage productivity and inventiveness, but where there are winners there are also losers. The values of the market—self-reliance, materialism, and consumerism—promote unbalanced ways of relating to others and relegate those without the skills that the market values to underemployment or poverty. For so-called minority groups, the pressure to adopt the values of the dominant culture is a double-edged sword. If African Americans and others do not participate in the larger economy, they will remain impoverished. If they assimilate completely, they lose themselves.

Hansberry's play provides a model of a middle way, a way in which people can preserve their identity while attending to their material needs. Through Moma, Hansberry promotes the strategy of double consciousness, a way of relating to the economic structures that avoids the pitfalls of total assimilation but maintains the individualism of the relational refugee. Such strategies require, but also enable, African Americans to affirm their faith and racial-ethnic heritage while participating fully in the pursuit of the American dream. By adopting a double consciousness, African Americans avoid the loss of identity entailed in assimilation by affirming what Archie Smith calls black history and culture, while still making a living in the capitalist economic system.[5]

The balancing act of double consciousness is both an unavoidable reality of African American experience and a skill that can be learned and honed. Those who would help African Americans as well as others whose attitude toward the market threatens them with alienation from their truest selves, need to mentor their charges in double consciousness.

The first task of the mentor is to facilitate critical reflection on the nature of the market economy and the economic problems facing African American people in particular. The values of consumer capitalism need to be clearly articulated and compared with the values of the community's heritage. Archie Smith writes:

> The mainstream with its materialistic and utilitarian values is a central part of the problem we must address on the path to any reordering of our personal and institutional lives. It is, therefore, necessary

to interpret personal and family difficulties in the light of an interpretation of how United States society as a whole works. It is the workings of this mainstream as a whole and our responses to it that give meaning to our experience. The deepening of meaning or purpose in life is the goal.[6]

The spiritual resources of African American traditions limit the extent to which we can participate in mainstream society by counterbalancing society's lure of self-interest. We must participate in the larger economy if we are going to survive, but we do not participate without a critical consciousness, an abiding loyalty to our family, race, and heritage.

The mentor also needs to set the clash in values in its larger context, in the fundamental differences in worldview that exist between the community's spiritual heritage and the market's materialism. Prosperity at any cost is a message to be rejected. We have large claims upon us that direct our economic values:

> Do not store up for yourselves treasures on earth, where moth and rust consume and where thieves break in and steal; but store up for yourselves treasures in heaven, where neither moth nor rust consumes and where thieves do not break in and steal. For where your treasure is, there your heart will be also. (Matthew 6:19-21)

On the practical level, the mentor must support those who are learning the skills of double consciousness in several ways. First, support systems must be established for men and women like Walter Lee, who have suffered defeat and humiliation in the economic sphere whether because of their own naïveté or the vagaries of the market. Second, the mentor should create forums where people learn about the structures of the economy and learn skills they will need to evaluate their career plans. Third, the mentor needs to publicize, in a variety of media, stories of people who have successfully handled the balancing act of double consciousness in the economic sphere and in other spheres of life. Finally, those who embark on the life of double consciousness in the marketplace will need resources to support them in this exhausting but rewarding task.

Of special significance are the needs of men like Walter Lee, who pursue get-rich-quick schemes that result only in further impoverishment. William Oliver has described the circumstances that lead to such self-defeating strategies and has named the trap "the philosophy of compulsive masculinity."[7] Marginalized men have organized ruthless and, for the most part, hopeless economic strategies because of their unfamiliarity with mainstream structures and opportunities. These men need contact with other mainstream people, especially other males, so that they can develop realistic and sustainable strategies for supporting themselves. Unemployed or underemployed men are at great risk of becoming relational refugees in the current economic situation and need special attention by mentors and others in the community who can help them remain full participants in community.

Again, on the practical level, mentors might create forums in which successful African Americans help others who want to invest what money they have in meaningful ways. There are many legitimate financial planners and business investment guides that can help people like Walter Lee invest their money in appropriate ways. The practical theologian can help make this happen.

Of special concern are those who are the truly disadvantaged, who are not only on the fringes of the mainstream, but are also beaten down. I speak here of those on the "unemployable" lists. They do not have the requisite resources that they need emotionally or educationally to do well in society. Mentors must identify and reach out to the endemically poor. There are programs that exist that actually work very well with these persons. One such program that has survived the federal budget cuts of the 1970s and 1980s is Reverend Leon Sullivan's program. Sullivan's Opportunities Industrialization Centers, a network of community-based skills training programs, has helped more than 1.5 million people in one hundred cities and eighteen countries find productive employment. In this age of limited welfare benefits, such programs are becoming even more critical to create, strengthen, and sustain.

Economic relational refugees suffer universally from low self-esteem and despair. People who have been counted out need a great deal of emotional and support system help. They need to be surrounded by people who care and want them to succeed in what they are doing. Mentors must provide positive experiences that reinforce the relational refugee's sense of self, in addition to teaching the skills that will enable them to negotiate the mainstream work world. The practical theologian needs to make sure these kinds of programs exist.

Conclusion

This chapter explored the economic factors that encourage people to become relational refugees. Both those who are most successful and those defeated by the market are at great risk. The double consciousness of African Americans is a helpful strategy for all those who want to preserve their truest identity and communal heritage while earning a meaningful living. Those who fail to develop double consciousness are vulnerable to becoming relational refugees. Those who remain grounded in their particular traditions of faith and culture can instead function as pilgrims, true to their God, true to their native land.

CHAPTER SIX

GRANDPARENTING AND THE RELATIONAL REFUGEE

Talk about the breakup of the family, about the need to return to family values, about the threat to the social order of single-parent homes and other shifts in family composition is common throughout our culture today. The changes that have occurred in the last few decades regarding whom we live with and how we are related are profound. The implications for the quality of our life, our self-understanding, and our moral compass are numerous. My concern in this chapter is neither to explain nor to judge the changes but to note a neglected aspect of family life in contemporary society, the increase in the number of grandparents who have a primary role in raising their grandchildren.

As we have seen, there are many types of relational refugees. In families headed by grandparents, three levels of refugees are evident. Grandparents are awarded custody of their grandchildren when the child's parents are absent or unable to provide adequate care. In such a situation, the natural parents are often relational refugees, persons so overwhelmed, unprepared, or inadequate that the even closest bonds of nature do not hold. The children, abandoned or neglected, are certainly at great risk but can be incorporated into new family structures in which they can flourish. The grandparents who happily comply or regretfully step in are more often reluctant mentors than refugees, but many grow frustrated and fatigued, placing both their own and the children's well-being at risk.

Some grandparents complain bitterly about this unfair imposition. They raised their own children and completed that phase of life. To return again to the demands of child rearing is difficult and exhausting. When the cause is the failure of one's own children to take responsibility for their offspring the frustrations mount. Many simply feel trapped. The dream of a restful period of relaxation following retirement evaporates.

The phenomenon of grandparents functioning as parents is not new. Perhaps it is unavoidable. There are many reasons why grandparents might have to step in as parents: the death of the parents, extraordinary job demands, and extended family systems that make such arrangements customary. I remember in the late 1970s reading autobiographies of African American seminarians at the Interdenominational Theological Center. I recall vividly that their grandparents, particularly their grandmothers, raised a large number of them.

The African American community has a proud history of extended family arrangements. Child-rearing responsibilities have been spread over several generations and across the boundaries of nuclear families, both out of necessity and out of a conviction, now lauded by many in our society, that "it takes a village" to raise a child.[1] It is clear that grandparents have been contributing their time, wisdom, and energy in the rearing of children since Africans were first brought to this country. However, grandparents who find themselves in this role today do not have the same support available as did previous generations. For most, the extended family is not as broad or as deep as it used to be. The aunts, uncles, neighbors, and friends who shared the work before are now no longer available to help. In many instances, elders now have to carry on with these unexpected and burdensome responsibilities on their own.

In addition, it appears that the number of grandparents who parent is increasing today, fueled by social conditions that make it difficult for parents to be parents. Don Browning notes that many people today feel they did not receive adequate parenting and so search to be re-parented in therapy or to self-parent, what he calls "self-psychology."[2] Whatever the hard numbers and causes, the visibility of grandparents who serve as parents is increasing, and the need to support them, their children, and their grandchildren is evident.

The Third Life of Grange Copeland

Alice Walker made grandparenting a major theme of one of her novels. In Walker's *Third Life of Grange Copeland,* the main character ends up, in the latter stages of his life, with custody of his grand-daughter. The story follows him both before and after this life-changing choice, through the tragic circumstances of his three lives. At the novel's end, Grange, a relational refugee, transforms himself into a heroic figure in order to save his own granddaughter from a tragic fate.[3] I am interested in the dynamics behind Grange's transformations, to judge if these transformations can serve as models for helping relational refugees.

In his first two lives, Grange plays the roles of the deadbeat dad and the street hustler. Walker underscores that Grange's abandon-ment of his children has its roots in cycles of bad parenting within the African American community that reach back to the destruc-tion of the nuclear family in slavery. Slave owners routinely broke up families as one mechanism to keep slaves under control. The destruction of the family system by racism led to poor parenting, which in turn leads to more poor parenting. This is only half of the story of African American families but it is an important part.

Grange became a street hustler in order to survive. As a young black man in the South, society did not offer him preparation for less dangerous and predatory work. He simply picked a role that the wider society expected him to play.

To escape the racism of the South, his own dead-end choices, and his past, Grange heads to New York. He expects to find oppor-tunity, freedom, and a chance for independence. He is bitterly disappointed, however. He finds that whites are just as much in control in the North as in the South and the same constraints apply to him.

Despite all this, on the run in the North, he somehow finds him-self. He finds what Archie Smith has called "self-reflexivity."[4] This transformation has three distinct stages. First, Grange changes his geographic and social location, disrupting the destructive patterns of his first life. Second, he develops, in Smith's words, "the capacity for solitude, conjuring, critical thinking, seeing oneself through the eyes of another, introspection, and self-correction."[5] Grange discovers that he has more choices regarding how he will live his life than he had previously thought, that he has the agency to act "with intent or purpose and with the belief that one can produce an effect or influence an outcome."[6] He is able to turn from being a refugee towards some semblance of community, which is the third stage.

Grange comes to his senses as a result of one of the most dramatic scenes in the novel. While walking through a park in New York City, Grange witnesses a white couple in the midst of a traumatic breakup. The woman is pregnant by the man but he has just revealed that he is married to another woman. He offers her money and leaves. She walks away from the money and leaves behind the ring he had given her as well. Grange approaches her in hopes that he can convince her to at least keep the money that she will obviously need. But she will not accept advice from the likes of him. No matter how low she might feel, despising him makes her feel a notch above somebody. She walks away across thin ice that gives way. Grange tries to save her. She takes his hand but a moment later lets go and drowns. Apparently, she prefers to die rather than allow herself to be saved by a black man. The last word she utters is "nigger."

In this scene, Grange learns the power of hate. He witnesses hate's ultimate end: self-destruction. He knows how to hate himself. He has found that the only way to survive in the world is to hate. And yet, he knows hate is not all he must do. He must also love. But, he will love only a few. He will love in an isolated and isolating way. When Grange gets custody of his granddaughter, Ruth, he tries to build a private world for the two of them. He discovers love's power but confines it in a defensive and protective manner that he cannot sustain. Without support from an extended family system, this grandparent's energy fails.

The relationship with Ruth is the key to free him from his status as a refugee but this one relationship alone is not enough. Grange's son, a man who also never received the parental support he needed, returns to claim Ruth. He has killed Ruth's mother, but nonetheless is again awarded custody. In an act of utter desperation, Grange shoots his own son in the courtroom rather than allow him to take custody of Ruth. Killing his own son, Grange goes to jail and Ruth is completely abandoned. So close to reimaging the world and the creative possibilities of life, Grange chooses despair. Murder is always a loss of faith.

Transformation of a Relational Refugee

The story of Grange Copeland teaches us many things about relational refugees. Grange nearly escapes the trap of refugee status but finally succumbs to a violent and self-destructive solution to the challenges he faced. Both his transformation and the ultimate failure of his conversion hold lessons for those who would respond to the predicament of relational refugees.

First, as I have outlined, Grange undergoes a three-step transformation. He changes locations from South to North. His journey is geographical, social, and emotional. His wanderings are like those of the ancient Israelites in the wilderness, a long process of re-formation in preparation for entry into the promised land. Like those ancient tribes, Grange learns slowly and backslides frequently. Grange's largest failing is his individualism. He never learns of his need for multileveled relationship and community support. He let Ruth into his world—and only her—but that was not enough to sustain the two of them as liberated individuals or together as a family.

Second, in Grange, hate and distrust beget hate and distrust. Grange was abandoned by his parents and so abandons both his son and, as a consequence of his despair, Ruth, who he has valiantly tried to save. Grange has felt the hatred of racist whites and the structures of racism. He learns to hate as well. He concludes that those who think others are good are simply naive. He eschews the role of trusting innocent. In the end, his distrust of his own son, perhaps justified, ultimately destroys the whole family.

Third, Grange nearly escapes the cycles that keep him from achieving liberated growth, through his relationship with Ruth. Walker seems to imply that relying on a grandchild for rescue from refugee status may be asking too much. Refugees need support in order to recover from their pain and return to community. In my reading, Grange genuinely cared for Ruth and sought to provide her with the nurture she required. His ultimate failure came not because he required too much of her, but instead, because he was not able to establish a network of support for the two of them. Relational refugees need to rejoin a web of community, a village, to complete their conversion and healing.

Strategic Intervention

Practical theology's function is to design strategic interventions, which take seriously some of the insights generated in the above analysis. The grandparents who are raising their grandchildren have many needs to which the practical theologian must attend.

Mentors must keep in mind the larger context in which these grandparents function. Responses must not only deal with specific families but address the wider cultural shifts as well. The first concern is to break the cycles of inadequate parenting that now exist in many communities. Like Grange and his son, those who do not receive adequate parenting, do not adequately parent. Practical theologians, pastors, and other mentors must address, in a variety of forums, the wider issues that contribute to the growing need for grandparents to step in as primary caregivers. Some examples include teenage pregnancy, high divorce rates, the poverty of most single-parent households, and the scourges of drug abuse, AIDS, and violence that increase the mortality of young parents.

Grandparents also need emotional and spiritual resources to sustain themselves, at an advanced age, for the momentous task of raising children. Most grandparents called to this task, unlike Grange, are not crippled as relational refugees, but rather are mature caregivers with open and generous hearts. Still, they need spiritual and emotional resources that are embedded in community. Despair can result from the exhaustion and isolation that accompanies child rearing and is a great threat to the well-being of both the elders and their charges. The task of mentors is not so much to rescue relational refugees as to build networks that sustain those who are committed to breaking through isolation and abandonment.

There are programs existing that embody some of the principles espoused in this chapter. The best of these programs are grounded in a hopeful expectation that investing one's energy in the future of youth is a privilege. Leaders do not have to be defensive about encouraging elders to take responsibility for the nurture of children at risk. In this age of abandoned and neglected children there is little choice. However, at the same time, mentors must serve as models and embrace all aspects of life, its ups and its downs, to empower and support those who agree to this momentous task. Such programs must also help grandparents realize that they need the village's support in the raising of their children and should not hesitate to ask for it.

One such program, mentioned in chapter 3, is the Ecumenical Families Alive Project developed by Professor Anne Streaty Wimberly, Ph.D. at the Interdenominational Theological Center. The mission of EFAP is to be a seminary-based service outreach initiative, in collaboration with faith and social support communities. EFAP provides two basic types of services. First, the program identifies and trains volunteers from the seminary community and from local congregations who are available to assist grandparents raising grandchildren and parents with troubled youth in the Atlanta Metro and Heard/Troup County areas. Second, the program provides service and learning opportunities for Interdenominational Theological Center students. Since October 1997, the staff and volunteers have hosted several forums in order to gather data about and provide support to grandparents who are raising grandchildren. The program trains volunteers to visit the homes of participating grandparents and to provide phone support services. It is crucial that the practical theologians support this and similar programs and create new ones for grandparents.

Conclusion

Grandparents do not have to feel isolated and alone as they undertake the task of raising grandchildren. Our culture encourages us to go it alone. Unable to overcome their fear of appearing inadequate or letting go of their image of autonomy, many grandparents find themselves overwhelmed by these new responsibilities. At the role level, grandparents find support among others engaged in the same activities. At the scene level, the opportunity to attend special activities and learn new skills assists grandparents in their efforts to make the experiences of their grandchildren meaningful. Finally, at the attitudinal level, the program enables grandparents to be less frustrated and burdened down, as well as to care for their own needs that accompany the aging process. Support from programs like those described and from other relatives, church communities, and the like makes grandparents who parent more emotionally available for their grandchildren.

Such practical programs need to be instituted on a wider basis. The supportive networks that we need, the village, is breaking down, but we do not have to accept this trend toward isolation. While we work to re-create community on a grand scale, we can periodically reconstitute the village in small ways, such as in programs that support grandparents who have had to take on the function of absent fathers and mothers, aunts and uncles. In fact, we must do so, if we want to end the cycle of inadequate parenting and the creation of future generations of relational refugees.

CHAPTER SEVEN

DRUG ADDICTION, SURROGATE FATHERS, AND THE RELATIONAL REFUGEE

Alice Childress's novel, *A Hero Ain't Nothin' But a Sandwich*, examines the stigma placed on those abandoned by their biological fathers.[1] This stigma is rooted primarily in the high value that the dominant culture places on the nuclear family. As we saw in the last chapter, defining a family exclusively as mom, dad, and two kids leaves many out and contributes to the creation of relational refugees among those who do not meet this standard.

African Americans have traditionally modeled proudly many family structures. Families based on stepparenting and informal and formal adoptions have been common in the African American community, according to Andrew Billingsley.[2] Unfortunately, the stigma that surrounds alternative families in this society encourages African Americans to downplay or ignore these important alternative structures for black families. It seems that the true legacy of the African American family, the strong extended family, is now, more than ever, under threat. Social policies, based on popular beliefs about the inadequacy of all but nuclear family households, removes support from poor, female-headed households as if they were the root of the problems of the black community rather than several hundred years of racism. It does appear that attitudes about the black family have permanently altered the way in which African Americans view their family relationships. This shift can be dated to the appearance of Daniel Patrick Moynihan's report, in the 1960s, on the black family.

Indeed, the Moynihan report blames single mothers and absentee fathers for the problems of African Americans. Moynihan's conclusions immediately stigmatized black, single-parent, and female-headed households. Overnight, the positive attitude toward matriarchal and extended family structures among African Americans was sharply eroded and replaced with a pejorative, culturally deviant understanding of black family life. In the black extended family, children were not stigmatized because their father was not a regular presence in their lives. Rather, all family members were treated as equal members of the larger whole, the extended kinship system. In the not so distance past, we could be proud that, as a race, our children were never orphaned and were always integrated into the community without stigma. Now, however, what was once our defining strength and legacy, has been added to the arsenal of prejudice against us.

For example, when I grew up in the 1940s, black preachers would include in the baptismal ceremonies of children of unwed mothers a statement rejecting the burdening of these children and their unmarried mothers with any stigma. To the contrary, these pastors proclaimed that such persons were equal members of God's family because, ultimately, God is the true father of all. Thus, the creative theology of our traditions muted the power of the label, "bastard." Being a child of a deadbeat dad, or being abandoned by a biological father, or being the son or daughter of an unwed mother did not generally cause black children to hate themselves and lead lives of self-destruction.

Richard Wright's fictional autobiography, *Black Boy,* provides a pre-Moynihan account of the development of a black, male, youth whose father abandoned the family. As a result, Wright and his mother were impoverished and had to depend on the generosity of a variety of relatives, necessitating frequent relocation. Wright's character certainly has a difficult life, but does not seem to suffer the self-hatred and loss of self-esteem that characterizes many children and youth that grow up in single-parent households today. In fact, Wright seems to have responded to his circumstances with a self-assertive personality with which he challenges the expectations placed upon him by a racist culture. He becomes stronger, not weaker.

Wright's strong Black Boy contrasts sharply with Benji, the main character in Alice Childress's *A Hero Ain't Nothin' But a Sandwich.* Benji is completely devastated by his father's abandonment of the family. At age thirteen, he becomes a heroin addict, a path of self-destruction chosen at least in part because he blames himself for his father's leaving. In this novel, the child fulfills Moynihan's prediction that children of female-headed households cannot develop into healthy and productive citizens. Benji is stigmatized and, in turn, fulfills the stereotypes that underlie the stigma.

It appears to me, then, that there was a monumental shift between the way a black child evaluated himself or herself after the Moynihan report. Moynihan promoted the stigmatization of black single and female-headed households by labeling family structures that were traditional among African Americans as African survivors, and creative responses to the attack upon the black family in slavery and beyond as culturally deviant. As a result, children of such families were made to feel defective. Even more important, creators of social programs became convinced that children from such homes were irredeemable. For those who could not resist this onslaught, their life was essentially over before it began. Such persons became relational refugees.

In this chapter, I focus on the interrelated problems of the erosion of self-esteem among young people who are raised in single-parent families and the self-destructive behavior that so often follows. To do this, I turn to Childress's novel, to uncover and evaluate her analysis of this problem and then to glean lessons for those who are involved in mentoring such young people. In *A Hero Ain't Nothin' But a Sandwich*, Childress describes how a black youth might overcome the shame and stigma of being abandoned by a biological father. Her answer is that a surrogate father, who relates to the young person with an attitude of persistent and selfless love, can save a child from self-destruction.

The Social Setting of Contemporary Society

It is clear to me that the decision to focus on the ways in which black families deviate from the norms of the wider society serves primarily as a distraction from problems which face all families in the United States. The phenomenon of children growing up without fathers is a problem of our society as a whole and not one that affects African Americans alone. It may be that African American families, weakened by years of discrimination and racism, illustrate more quickly and dramatically than white families the effects of wider societal shifts, such as the trend from dual-parent to single-parent households. Nonetheless, what black families face is common to all families.

For example, several general observations can be made about the post-Moynihan family. First, there appears to have been a shift in the deep metaphors that inform our lives from a Freudian view of human growth and development, as reflected in the Oedipal myth, to Browning's approach based on the myth of Telemachus. Following the story of Oedipus, Freud concluded that boy children seek to drive fathers from the home because they block the son's access to the mother. The son views his father as a competitor. The tension is resolved when the son, fearing the father's retaliation if he were to fulfill the forbidden wish to possess his mother, appeases the father by identifying with him. This Freudian scenario is being replaced today. Don Browning has proposed that the myth of Telemachus fits our present circumstances better than the Oedipal story.[3] In this story, the son is abandoned by his biological father and raised by surrogates. Through this change in metaphors, Browning suggests that we must change our view of human nature.

It seems that this post-Freudian and post-Moynihan age is characterized by a form of rootlessness or homelessness. Some analysts emphasize flaws in the individual as the primary cause of this shift, using the label "narcissism." I reverse the sense of causation, noting the effect of the rootlessness on individual development, on the creation within this social context of relational refugees. That is, people feel isolated, cut off from society. This isolation erodes self-esteem, resulting in the feeling that one is unloved and unlovable. This, in turn, creates a destructive tension within the self where one feels acutely the need to be loved, while at the same time one is fearful of entering close relationships with others. According to Browning, this has led to a shift from Freudian psychological models to a form of self-psychology, object relations theory, and shame psychology. These psychological approaches focus on the pervasive sense of shame that people feel as the result of being cut off from others. Since isolation is so pervasive in our society, we are all at risk of succumbing to shame. Benji's crisis is a potential crisis for us all. Childress's fictional reflections on overcoming the shame of abandonment addresses a general problem of the entire society.

Benji as A Relational Refugee

Childress's book is about a thirteen-year-old drug addict who is convinced that he is worthless because his biological father left him. Although he is surrounded by many people who love and care for him, including a grandmother, several teachers, and some of his peers, he cannot accept their love. At the same time, he desperately wants to be loved. On one occasion, he admits that he wished he had one friend, "one who dig me the most and don't put anybody else ahead of me."[4] But he remains convinced that he is all alone in the world, that no one really cares for him. He goes on to berate himself for ever having expected someone to care for him. He refuses to believe that anyone could really care about him since his own father did not.

Craig Butler loved Rose Johnson, Benji's mother. He wanted to marry her, but he could not since she had never pursued a divorce from Benji's father. Craig, a struggling maintenance man, takes a real interest in Benji. He is willing to play the role of surrogate father for Benji, to help him recover a sense of self-worth. In response, Benji rebuffs him. Benji warns Craig that saving him is hopeless, that he does not merit such a heroic effort, that in any case, "a hero ain't nothin' but a sandwich."

Resentful that Craig lives with his mother without benefit of marriage, Benji devises a plan to remove Craig from his mother's life. He steals Craig's suit and overcoat and uses the money to buy drugs. Craig gets the message and moves out of the apartment. But he does not move out of the apartment building. He just moves downstairs to another woman's apartment. Benji, not yet satisfied, devises another plan to force Craig out of the building. One day he breaks into the apartment where Craig has taken up residence. He steals the toaster. Craig hears him and gives chase. Craig is enraged with Benji for this belligerent act and wants to punish him with a beating. Benji runs to the top of the apartment building where he tries to escape by jumping from one rooftop to another. When his leap falls short, Craig reaches out and grabs Benji to keep him from falling six stories to his death. Benji tries desperately to free himself so he will fall and end his miserable life. Craig holds on. Benji struggles hard but cannot free himself from Craig's viselike grip. Craig injures his arm and legs while maintaining his hold, but still refuses to let go. Finally, Benji allows Craig to reel him in. Benji at last realizes that Craig has risked his life to save him, that Craig is truly a hero—and not just a sandwich either.

After the rescue, Benji holds onto Craig on that rooftop. He understands that in Craig he has finally received the answer to his prayers. He is finally convinced that someone loves him.

Craig's heroic action reaffirms the black tradition of fictive kin and informal adoption. Craig is not Benji's biological father but his love breaks through Benji's hard exterior. Benji, like many young people in the post-Moynihan era, is very suspicious of those who offer them care and want positive proof that it is genuine. Not until Craig risked his life for Benji did Benji believe he was cared for and loved. Indeed, it was selfless, unconditional, and nonreciprocal love that saved Benji that day.

The Self as Damaged Goods

Benji saw himself as damaged goods. Abandoned by his father, he saw himself as unworthy of another's care and love. As we have seen, he eventually sank low enough to want to end his miserable life. His own assessment of himself and his crippled self-image are instructive.

Benji felt as if he had reared himself from the age of five or six. In his opinion, by the time you are seven or eight, adults are so busy with their own lives that they do not have time for needy and dependent children. He understood that he had to fend for himself. Benji took on an air of toughness to compensate for his deep, unmet need for adult and parental guidance. He felt that he could not trust adults with his vulnerable side, that he could not cry or reveal that he felt sorry for himself. Instead, he did his best to show the world that he could manage without parental love. In fact, one of the reasons behind his initial experimentation with heroin was to show his peers how fearless he was. Of course, underneath, he was a very scared and needy boy.

Things were not always as difficult for Benji. At one point, he declares that he had a happy childhood, at least until Craig Butler came into the picture. Before Craig's entrance into the family, Benji felt secure because he had his mother all to himself. He was the center of attention with both his mother and his grandmother. His mother was happy then as well, according to Benji. In fact, he saw himself as his father's able replacement, as the man of the house. Craig disrupted his special position in relation to his mother. Talking about the relationship between Craig and his mother, Benji says:

> But all of a sudden I'm wonderin in my mind, what they need with me? What they need with Grandma? What they need with anybody? I feel like a accident that happen to people. My blood father cut out on Mama. Musta gone cause he didn't dig me. Mama look at me lotta times and say, "My God, you look just like Big Benny, just like him." Her eyes be sad when she say it.[5]

The loss of his mother's full attention set Benji on the road to decline. In response, he laid out the intricate plans to push Craig out of his mother's life.

Benji's words reveal that his father's leaving and Craig Butler's arrival into his mother's life were central and painful experiences from which he had not yet recovered. No doubt, these scenes and related perceptions, and his feelings about them, encouraged him to interpret his life in a tragic way. I would also suggest, however, that his mother's tendency to look at him and see his father also contributed to his decline. Childress reveals very little about Benji's biological father, leaving the reader to wonder about him. All that we know about the father is summed up in one of Benji's monologues. However, it appears that his mother confined Benji within her image of her first husband. This oft repeated scene appears to have scripted Benji as a pathetic character in a hopeless plot.

As if his circumstances and his mother's response to them were not enough, Benji also had to face the wider society's stigmatization of children who come from broken and female-headed households. This combination of factors communicated to Benji that he was unacceptable and unlovable. It is no wonder that he distrusted genuine love and would be suspicious of anyone who offered it. In fact, had it not been for the "miracle on the rooftop," it appears that Benji would have been lost forever. Had it not been for Craig's heroic intervention, it is likely that Benji would have died of a drug overdose.

Theological Themes in Childress's Novel

Childress makes no attempt to present a full-scale theology within her novel but offers the practical theologian some materials on which we must reflect. Benji's grandmother, Mrs. Ransom Bell, introduces what I take to be Childress's central proposition—that God is an incarnational God who gets intimately involved in the lives and affairs of human beings. Mrs. Bell describes Jesus as her personal savior, the Son of God, and a "waymaker."[6] By waymaker, Mrs. Bell means that God is present in the midst of the frustrations of life. For her, God is an ever-present help among evil human enemies, in times of lack of shelter, when loved ones are indifferent or even cruel, during the aging process, and when one is the victim of street violence. She says: "Even in the midst of my heartache, light shines in my soul, and I am truly lifted! The walls of this little room just roll back, and bright glory shines everywhere, in my heart, in the air; round the mirror glass on the wall turns glinty and sparkly, and a glassa water is a glassa diamonds!"[7]

Less explicit, but more important to my task here, is Childress's portrayal of Craig Butler as a savior figure. On the rooftop, Craig Butler literally holds Benji's life in his hands. As he holds tightly onto Benji's hand, Craig reflects in a manner reminiscent of Jesus in the Garden of Gethsemane. As he prepared to walk the Way of the Cross, Jesus struggled with his ambivalence, wondering whether he was equal to the assigned task. He cried: "Abba, Father, for you all things are possible; remove this cup from me; yet, not what I want, but what you want" (Mark 14:36). Craig, too, came to realize that the task of surrogate fatherhood was very difficult and perhaps not a cup from which he would choose to drink. Craig was tempted to abandon his mission much in the same way that Jesus was, and in the same way Benji's actual father did. Then, like Jesus, Craig also had a sudden revelation. He knew that he would not even be thinking this way if Benji were his flesh and blood. He would not have tucked tail and run when things got tough between

Benji and him, if Benji had been his own son. It was this sudden realization that caused Craig to adopt Benji in his heart, to pull him back onto safe ground, and to hold him and not let him go.

Whereas I do not doubt or disdain the heroism of Christ, Childress's portrayal of Craig in messianic terms presents a problem for me. I want to encourage the rescue of abandoned children, but I do not want to set up a counterproductive standard of heroism for those who undertake the task of serving as surrogate fathers. Childress's story promotes an individualistic heroism characteristically emphasized in the history of the United States. Benji required a dramatic rescue. However, such heroism is very limited in its impact and is inadequate without being a part of larger networks of support within the community, the village. Whereas we must be vigilant so that children do not fall off of rooftops or through the cracks, it is as important to reconstruct the village and the extended family. It is a communal responsibility to shepherd youth through the maze of adolescence. Such a function is certainly indispensable today, and the church is the appropriate institution to undertake it. Unfortunately, throughout its history, the black church has proved itself woefully inadequate to the needs of black youth.[8]

Strategic Intervention

Two dominant themes emerge from my reflections on Childress's novel. First, African American children from female-headed households continue to endure devaluation and stigmatization. Second, individual heroism by African American surrogate fathers to save African American children is a crucial but inadequate response. It should be clear that I believe any devaluation of human beings, no matter who they are or where they come from, is ethically flawed and a sin. In addition, I contend that individualistic heroism on the part of African American males is welcomed, but woefully inadequate to respond to the actual needs of black children. Only when we recover a sense of communal caring for our adolescent children will we ultimately save them.

The Christian gospel makes clear that human standards of valuation are not ultimate. True worth is a gift from God. We are ultimately valued in God's sight, not in the eyes of other human beings. And we are valuable to one another not because of our status or role but because we are made in the image of God. Ethical systems that assign a higher value to people who live within certain family structures, a dual-headed nuclear family for instance, are, therefore, heretical. Our truest family is the family of God, not our human family, and especially no particular type of human family. All forms of human families must be judged in light of the eschatological family, which has a totally different standard of human valuation. In the eschatological family of God, worth and dignity are not the only gifts from God. The power to grow in grace is a gift from God as well. Consequently, practical theology needs to proceed from the truth that all people reflect God's image equally.

With this theological assumption firmly in place, I turn to the task of outlining strategies to follow for aiding children in their journey from relational refugees to liberated persons in community. First, I discuss the context in which this work takes place. Second, I propose a model of pastoral care that is dedicated to the reestablishment of supportive communities. Much of what I am about to say appears in my doctoral dissertation.[9] The return to these ideas is warranted by the current emphasis on the role of the church in pastoral care.[10]

Our society suffers profoundly from the deterioration of mediating structures. By mediating structures I refer to institutions such as the family, church, and voluntary association that both link and buffer the individual and the larger institutions of society.[11] These larger institutions are the political, economic, governmental, and educational suprastructures of society. Mediating structures are essential to human existence. In them, we find love, affirmation, expectations about our behavior, moral values, enabling narrative and plots, and other immaterial resources that give our lives purpose and meaning. The mediating structures provide the emotional and relational support for us to deal with the exigencies of life. In modern society, however, mediating structures have slowly been losing their ability to support the lives of individuals. Individuals appear to be standing naked before the large suprastructures with no intermediary institutions. Regarding this trend, I have written elsewhere:

> Although life goes on with a great deal of continuity within the black community, we are now under attack by the pervasive social and economic forces of the present. Many of the support structures

and traditions of the black church, which have been conveyers and custodians of past cherished values, are now feeling the slicing cut of the sharp blades of modern progress. We are stumbling into an era when traditional values will have less impact upon our lives as individuals, even when we remain vigilant to preserve these values.[12]

The task, then, for practical theologians is "to strengthen the mediating structures; namely the family, church, voluntary associations, neighborhoods, and subcultures."[13]

Most of the mentoring tasks I have outlined throughout this book were once accomplished routinely through these mediating structures. Without such structures, individuals have no buffer against negative values, narratives, and plots with which the wider society bombards them. Thus, African American youth become more vulnerable to developing a crippled self-esteem.

Religious support systems are especially important because they provide an overarching narrative that orients the individual in the cosmos. Through their theologies, stories, and rituals religious institutions tell us who we are in the deepest sense. Providing a sense of a coherent past and a promising future, religion helps us through both predictable and surprising transitions and crises of life. Finally, they enable a faith in God that heals, sustains, guides, and reconciles us in the midst of life's difficulties.[14]

In an effort to recover the communal dimensions of care, the practical theologian attempts to bring these support system resources to bear on our lives. Our tasks, then, as practical theologians, are many. We must lift up the significance of support systems and mediating structures for our lives. We must educate and train lay people to participate productively in support groups. We must learn to use, and teach others to use, the rituals and religious resources of the church for times of particular need. We also must continue to create and utilize conceptual tools, such as psychological theories that take seriously the development of human beings over the course of their lifetimes, cross-generational models of family life, and community models of mental health.[15] Finally, we must mobilize support systems in times of crisis.

There is a public, as well as therapeutic, dimension of our work as well. Public theologians who remind the public and the church that we need face-to-face communities to thrive as human beings, are essential. We must never allow ourselves to be captivated by an isolationist understanding of the individual. Instead, we need to help the public and the church to visualize a form of self-development and actualization that contributes to this same development in others.

The recovery of community is essential for our survival and for the rescuing of our young refugees. In the African village, aunts and uncles, rather than an individual heroic parent or grandparent, prepare the youth for initiation into adulthood. It takes the entire village. In our context, the church must take the place of the village. The church must rediscover its own traditional rites of initiation for our youth in order to assist them in the transition from adolescence to adulthood. Heroic parents, whether biological or surrogate, together with the caring community and support from the local church, will get this job done.

The construction of responses to the problem of drug addiction illustrates how I envision the role of the church in this context. It is clear to me that substance abuse is a form of medicating the wounds that have been inflicted in the absence of the traditional village support structures in contemporary society. We know it takes a village to raise a child but right now we have no village in which to do so. It is precisely the pain of isolation caused by the breakup of the traditional village that drugs seek to medicate. Drugs are a poor substitute for community.

The loss of community is the root of nihilism, rampant among the youth of today. The only real antidote for the lack of community is the restoration of community. Only the recovery of mediating structures, like the small church voluntary association and the extended family of both blood and fictive kin, can deal with the true source of the drug problem. Heroic parents are certainly needed but, without a total village effort, cannot succeed.

To respond to the drug problem, then, practical theologians must identify and develop programs that create the support systems of the village, in addition to attending to the individual addict. This is a problem that requires the participation of the entire community and all its institutions, especially the local black church. Individual pastoral counseling is only a stopgap measure. The entire local church must see this as its task.

One program that addresses wider, communal dimensions of issues surrounding the transition of youth into adulthood is called

Ella J. Baker House, run by a forty-eight-year-old ex-gang member, who attended Harvard and became a Pentecostal preacher. His name is Gene Rivers and he lives and works in Dorchester, Massachusetts. [16] The Ella J. Baker House embodies many of the principles outlined above. Baker House is a small village in the midst of urban violence and teenage malaise, where youth can find a home, a place to belong. It is a communal response, not an individualistic hero approach, to the needs of these young people. Rivers is no Lone Ranger but is assisted by many heroes and heroines who have left lucrative employment to serve the next generation.

The inspiration to establish the Baker House arose in the form of a tragic scene. In 1992, during the funeral of a gang member, in a Baptist church, a gang chased a boy into the church, then beat and stabbed him in front of a group of mourners. Rivers says this incident served as a wake-up call for ministers and churches to become an active and visible presence in a community that had been abandoned to the gangs and drugs. In an article about the program, a reporter writes:

> Now both sides are beginning to form an unlikely alliance founded on the idea that the only way to rescue kids from the seductions of the drug and gang cultures is with another, more powerful set of values: a substitute family for young people who almost never have two parents, and may not even have one, at home. And the only institution with the spiritual message and the physical presence to offer those traditional values, these strange bedfellows have concluded, is the church.[17]

Rivers has created a communal and holistic program as a response to something a drug pusher said to him one day. The pusher explained that God is losing the battle for the souls of inner-city youth because the pusher is present when Johnny goes to buy bread for his mother and the church is not. The pusher concludes: "I'm there, you're not. I win, you lose. It's all about being there."[18]

Indeed, it is all about who is there to replace the ancient village. Many people, including the government, are looking to faith-based programs for the answer to the problems of inner-city youth. We must remember, however, what Rivers and Childress have tried to teach us. Their work indicates that there is no substitute for the heroic commitment of individuals and groups if young people are to be saved. It will take people who are willing to give up the pursuit of the American dream and instead pursue structures as supportive and strong as the ancient African village, in order to win the day.

CHAPTER EIGHT

DYING WITH DIGNITY AND THE RELATIONAL REFUGEE

The subject of how to die with dignity is a universal human question. But in this age, when teenagers shoot their classmates, when courts debate physician-assisted suicides, when the AIDS crisis rages on, and when nations pursue genocidal policies of ethnic cleansing, the question is particularly pressing. In his Pulitzer Prize winning book, *The Denial of Death,* Ernest Becker painstakingly chronicles how modern people were preoccupied with the denial of death.[1] He contends that in previous generations we denied the reality of death because we feared death so profoundly. This denial was a central motivation for many of our choices and yet, he reminds us, death is inescapable and avoidance, futile. Today, it appears we have moved from denying the reality of death to embracing its reality. We seem more interested today in learning what dying has to teach about living.

I was reminded recently of how much the dying have to teach us about life. Two cases, in particular, have been seminal in shaping my current thinking. In both cases the role of community and family relationships is central in making both dying and living meaningful. The first case, which came to my attention in the form of a novel, involves a black man who was sentenced to death and executed after participating in a convenience store robbery that resulted in a murder.[2] The second case is about a father and his homosexual son who is dying of AIDS.

These two incidents taught me several important lessons. The first lesson is that God is at God's best in the midst of human suffering, pain, and dying. The second lesson is that the community, the small village, the informal caring network, is essential to human health and wholeness. Groups, places, settings where we are known, in which we care for one another, and are encouraged not to give up on loving others are essential for sustaining meaningful human lives. The third lesson is that the reality of death's inevitability does not preclude the possibility of human fulfillment. Rather, in the context of loving community, those facing death and those who love them can become fully present to each other, fully themselves, fully human.

The purpose of this chapter is to identify the benefits of the reconstruction of caring relationships characteristic of the small village, when death is inevitable. Many die alone in this era. Alienated or exiled from family, friends, and community the dying in a death denying culture are prime candidates to become relational refugees. The stories I reflect on here call us to reincorporate the dying, as well as the living, as we create community in this land of isolation.

Race, Sex, and Human Possibility

Racism infects the soul. Racism is an ideology rooted in a fear of scarcity—scarcity of value, scarcity of possibility. Oppressor groups limit access to social, political, and economic capital, afraid that there is not enough for people of all races to share. They do this by constructing myths and stereotypes to legitimate their own privilege while employing coercive power, actual or potential violence, to bar the so-called inferior group from opportunity. Wherever human beings construct value systems that assign some to categories of inferiority, both victim and perpetrator are diminished. The pernicious nature of racism attacks, from the inside out, those deemed inferior because of the color of their skin, eroding self-esteem. Like racism, homophobia defines people according to a hierarchy of value. Homophobia contends that a person's sexual preference and orientation disqualifies him or her from the status of full humanity. As we might expect, those who are considered less than fully human are also excluded from full participation in society. Homophobia denies gay men and lesbians full human dignity because those in power fear the unknown, the blurring of sexual boundaries, and the disorientation of reconsidering how the world might be structured if not on gender complementarity, traditional readings of scripture, and traditional understandings of the family. Homophobia, like racism, preserves the privilege of the powerful through myths and stereotypes that contain within them triggers of violence. Like racism, it denies its victims access to basic human rights. I agree with Archie Smith that many gay men and lesbians become relational refugees because they, in a manner not unlike that under which African Americans have suffered, are denied the opportunity to define themselves and are subject instead to messages of scorn, disgust, and disdain.[3]

At a keynote address at the American Association of Marriage and Family Therapy in Atlanta, Georgia, in October 1997, the Reverend Jesse Jackson was asked for his thoughts on homosexuality. Jackson replied, "gays and lesbians have a right to find love wherever they can." I hear in Jackson's words, as I would expect from a man who has dedicated his life to the struggle for equality, an affirmation of the dignity of all persons, without affirming all the particular ways people choose to live out their lives. Our basic need as human beings is to be affirmed in the midst of human community. Homophobia excludes gay men and lesbians from full participation in human community, placing them at risk of becoming relational refugees.

No human being wants to die alone. When we die, we want to be surrounded by loved ones. If it is not sudden, the process of dying offers an opportunity to strengthen our bonds with those whom we care about most. Unfortunately, racism and homophobia, but most especially the latter, have served as a barrier to this sense of connection in many families. AIDS has forced us to consider what is important at the time of death—our moral traditions or our human bonds of love. I have learned from people who live with and died from AIDS, both homosexual and heterosexual, that familial and communal bonds remain crucial to their well-being despite experiences of rejection and misunderstanding. As we prepare to say good-bye to loved ones, let us rely on these strong bonds rather than on our fears, for after all, we remain members of the same family, both the human family and the family of God.

Death and Race in *A Lesson Before Dying*

In his novel *A Lesson Before Dying* Ernest Gaines accepts that racism influences who gets the death penalty. In the context of pre–civil rights Louisiana, Gaines expects his protagonist, Jefferson, to be tried, convicted, and sentenced to death because he is a black man who was involved in a robbery during which a white person was killed. Gaines does not argue about the morality of capital punishment, nor does he focus obsessively on the innocence of a black man who was simply in the wrong place at the wrong time. Gaines's concern is, rather, whether it is possible for a black man on death row to change and what that transformation might mean to a community.

As the book opens, Jefferson awaits electrocution. Jefferson struggles to prepare himself for death. He draws upon the resources of his religious tradition in this process. He unashamedly connects his own death with that of Jesus. He is most impressed with Jesus' ability to die with dignity. Jefferson wants to face his own death with the same assurance with which the Good Friday spiritual describes Jesus, "He never said a mumbling word."[4]

Gaines's contribution as an author is to set Jefferson's predicament in its wider context. The population, with only a few exceptions, of the small town in Louisiana where Jefferson is imprisoned hopes for his transformation. First graders and sixth graders, whites and blacks, even the police officers hope that Jefferson changes before he dies in the electric chair. The destiny of the entire town seems to be linked to that of Jefferson. Everyone is hoping that before he dies he can move from a life of violence and hostility to one of dignity and compassion. Knowing the man who is about to be killed forces everyone in the town to think about what makes life meaningful. They agree it would be tragic for Jefferson to die and not know what it means to really care for someone.

Jefferson can barely write his name or read, but Grant Wiggins, a young African American school teacher, gives him a notebook and a pencil anyway. No one expects Jefferson to use the notebook, but the guards allow him to keep it, along with the pencil, and a small knife to sharpen the pencil. Although Jefferson does not have a good command of English, he puts his thoughts down on paper. Following his execution, the white jailers to whom Jefferson had entrusted his notebook share it with the public. The notebook records Jefferson's process of transformation. With no capital letters, no punctuation marks, and inaccurate spelling, Jefferson reveals, in detail, his inner shift from a person who thought of himself as an animal to one who cared about himself and others. His journal indicates that one event stands out as particularly meaningful in this process—the day when a group of children visited him.

One day Grant Wiggins surprised Jefferson by bringing his class for a visit.[5] Jefferson noticed right away how they had dressed up and cleaned up just to see him. He commented on how scared the children looked and how brave they were to come to see him. He was touched when his cousin Estel kissed him on his cheek. He wrote about how he could not hold back his tears.

After the children, many other visitors came. Jefferson was pleased. He recorded the names of all the visitors:

> Then after the chiren here com the ole folks an look like everbody from the quarter was here mis julia an joe an mis haret an ant agnes an mr noman an mis sara an mis lilia an mr harry an mis lena an god kno who all an mr ofal an mis felia wit her beeds an jus prayin an all the peple sayin how good i look an lord hav merce sweet jesus mr wigin how you got bok yer in that suit that suit look like it half bok siz cause i member mis rita got him that suit way back ten leben yers back an bok babbin ther like he kno me as mis rita sayin he want say he glad to see me. [6]

The climax of the day was the moment Jefferson received a gift from Buck, or in Jefferson's hand, bok. Buck, who had a mental disability, wanted to give Jefferson a present. He gave Jefferson the biggest marble he had in his pocket. A little while later, Buck wanted his big marble back, but he gave Jefferson another smaller one. Buck's generosity touched Jefferson deeply. Afterwards, Jefferson wrote:

> this was the firs time i cry when they lok that door bahind me the very firs time an i jus set on my bunk cryin but not let them see or yer me cause i didn want them think rong but i was cryin cause of bok an the marble he giv me and cause o the peple com to see me cause they hadn never done nothin lik that for me befor[7]

Through his story, Gaines confirms for us that even in the most dire situation, transformation remains a possibility. People can change even as they stare death straight in the face. A community can decide that it is possible to be humane and caring rather than vindictive. A man can decide to let himself feel love rather than let animal survival instincts dominate his life. Both Jefferson and the community decided to change, to fulfill their God given potential, to step out on faith, and show that they cared.

During his trial, Jefferson was referred to as a hog. He internalized this label. While on death row, he hardly said a mumbling word. When he did talk, he would say, "I'm a old hog. Youmans don't stay in no stall like this. I'm a old hog they fattening up to kill."[8] He had internalized the negative attitudes with which others had bombarded him all of his life. He simply came to believe what they said. He believed that he had no worth, no value.

Racism contributed to Jefferson's fate. He had violated the law by participating in the robbery. He had been present when the victim had been killed. But he had not done the killing. Jefferson was sentenced to death not because he was guilty, but because he violated the unwritten law that when a black person kills a white person a black life is required in retribution, no matter the circumstances.

The town did not reflect on this injustice. No one came to Jefferson's rescue in his moment of need. Perhaps they could not even imagine such a possibility. However, with few exceptions, the community desired that he die, not like a beast or an animal, but as a human being with a sense of dignity. The entire town seemed to want him to know, before he died, what it felt like to love and be loved. There seemed to be an underlying sympathy for Jefferson's plight.

Perhaps because Jefferson was a member of the community, the townspeople realized that they were executing one of their own. He was not just an anonymous black face but a young man that they all knew. This personal knowledge seemed to make the real difference. Everyone, including the judge and the public officials, as well as the black community, knew the circumstances of his life. They also knew and respected his godmother. Jefferson's godmother worked as a maid for one of the leading white figures of the community, and she was well respected. Therefore, they were executing one of their own who happened to go bad.

The lesson that Jefferson had to learn was that there was a role other than that of criminal that he could play in his life. The entire community wanted him to know, before he died, what it was like to play the role of a caring human being. Jefferson did not have to look far for worthy models to emulate. His godmother, his pastor, Grant Wiggins, and Paul, a prison guard, all provided him positive scenes in which they tried to communicate that he was a valued human being. The day when the children visited him, his cousin kissed him, and Buck gave him the marble was critical. He was moved to tears because he had never felt that kind of love in his life. Experiencing the love of his friends, family, and community, Jefferson would not die like an animal.

The most important scene, however, took place at the actual execution. Here Jefferson was the main actor on stage. This was his first and last act as a full human being. He came to die with dignity the way Jesus died. He came to die without saying a mumbling word. Paul, the guard, recounted the event:

"He was the strongest man in that crowded room, Grant Wiggins," Paul said, staring at me and speaking louder than was necessary. "He was, he was. I'm not saying this to make you feel good, I'm not saying this to ease your pain. Ask that preacher, ask Harry Williams. He was the strongest man there. We all stood jammed together, no more than six, eight feet away from that chair. We all had each other to lean on. When Vincent asked him if he had any last words, he looked at the preacher and said, 'Tell Nannan I walked.' And straight he walked, Grant Wiggins. Straight he walked. I'm a witness. Straight he walked."[9]

Strategic Intervention

Now that the First Lady of our nation, Hillary Clinton, has popularized it, we hear everywhere that "it takes a village to raise a child." I would like to expand the scope of this popular phrase to "it takes a village to make a whole person." By village, I mean those small community networks of care and support that help us maintain our emotional and physical well-being as we go through life's major transitions and crises.[10] Ernest Gaines's novel helps us to see just how the village is essential in facilitating the development of whole persons. It is the love and affection of the entire village or neighborhood that facilitates Jefferson's transformation. It is the functioning of the village at every mimetic level—plot, role, scene, and attitude—that facilitates every person's wholeness.

Gaines's novel tells us that we should never give up on anyone. This was the attitude of Jesus, and this was the attitude of Jefferson's community. If we have this attitude, we will refuse to let anyone become a relational refugee. If we never give up on anyone, we will live as a village, a village that imitates Jesus' all-embracing hospitality.

Homosexuality, Propositional Ethics, and Death

One way for villages, small communities, and local congregations to become places that facilitate wholeness and keep people from becoming relational refugees is to adopt a dynamic, narrative-based ethical approach. The gospel calls us to enact and live out the salvation drama of God and not rely on a propositional approach to the ethics of ministry. A propositional approach to ministry focuses on the establishment and enforcement of rules and regulations. Following this approach, pastors and church communities expend their energy making sure that people live by these rules. Such rules are necessary if the village is to survive and thrive, but they are not the only means of building community.

Biblically, Christian ethics rely on the spirit and not the letter of the law. Jesus said the law will not pass away without being fulfilled but also that the law was made for humanity and not humanity for the law. In other words, for Christians, there is a relational dimension to living in the village that goes deeper than the laws.

Christian ethical reflection, at its most fundamental level, is based not on propositions but on narratives, stories. We need rules to make communities function smoothly, but on a deeper level the communities are constituted, formed, and shaped by story. Put most simply, story shapes our character.[11] In this approach, pastors, counselors, and church members expend their energy telling the community's stories, acting in accordance with these stories, and encouraging others to internalize the stories as well. The goal is not to enforce rules, but to get people to identify with the dominant stories of the community and to shape their behavior based on the leading characters that are portrayed in the stories. Propositional character comes as a result of conforming to the law, whereas, narrative character emerges as a result of embracing the stories of the faith community and living them out.[12]

When confronted by the issue of homosexuality, many churches respond only with the propositional model. "The Bible says it's wrong and that's that" is a common retort. On the whole, the black church is committed to a heterosexual norm for human relationships. Most understand the Bible to say that to live faithfully as a Christian is to enter a heterosexual marriage covenant or to remain celibate. As a consequence, the choice to enter into a same-sex relationship is a failure, wrong, or even sinful. Yet, many local black churches go beyond this exclusivity, quietly embracing gay men and lesbians in their midst. Such churches generally do not condone homosexual practice, but they affirm the dignity and worth of homosexuals as God's children.

In the churches in which I grew up, most people agreed that homosexuality was a private concern between God and the person. We treated everybody, including gay men and lesbians, fairly, as fellow members of God's family. At the same time, in official documents and doctrines, in preaching, and elsewhere, it was clear that heterosexuality was the norm and that the practice of homosexuality was a sin, inconsistent with the practices of the Christian faith.[13] As a result, people kept their sexual preferences hidden as much as they could, enduring the ambiguity of this strained hospitality.

There are those, however, who warn that hostility toward gay men and lesbians is growing in some quarters of the black church. Archie Smith decries the fact that any person, including homosexuals, are excluded from the black church and made homeless refugees.[14] He contends that propositional views that are exclusive, restrictive, and punitive are gaining ascendancy in many African American churches.

The approach to homosexuality I am recommending is intended to balance the biblical tradition and the history of interpretation among African Americans with a commitment to show hospitality to all God's children, to refuse to make anyone a relational refugee. My position bridges the two categories of rejection nonpunitive and qualified acceptance in Larry Graham's model of approaches to the issue of homosexuality in the churches.[15]

The rejection nonpunitive approach accepts the heterosexual norm for sexual behavior while recognizing that homosexuals are children of God belonging to God's family. In other words, it embraces the sinner but rejects the sin. The qualified acceptance orientation accepts the fact that neither Jewish nor Christian scholars have reached a consensus regarding biblical and theological norms for homosexuality. It also concedes that scientific evidence about the health and morality of homosexual practice is inconclusive. In other words, until a consensus emerges calling for the full embrace or exclusion of gay men and lesbians, the church should show its characteristic hospitality.

Combining these approaches in my strategies for mentoring, I embrace the experiences of those who are gays and lesbians, while maintaining the standard of a heterosexual norm. What is important is to value all people equally, to welcome the stranger, to overcome alienation within the Body of Christ, who reconciles all things.

An excellent example of the narrative orientation at work is reported in the book entitled *AIDS* by Shelp, Sunderland, and Mansell.[16] In it, they report a case of a father who belonged to a black Pentecostal denomination and was committed to the propositional approach to Christian ethics of sexuality. This man's son was gay and contracted AIDS along with his lover. Even though his own ethical system counted his son among the damned, the father refused to exclude the son or his lover from the family. This man saw his son as his son, as a member of the family, as a member of the family of God. The man's church gave the man a difficult time. They did not think he should accept who his son was because his son had acted in opposition to the church's rules and practice. However, the father refused to make his son a relational refugee. At an earlier point, he and his son had a falling out over the son's sexual orientation. His son told him that the family had become a source of pain rather than support. So, now, when facing his own child's death, the man refused to allow his son to die without reaching out to him.

For me, this father's attitude represents the best response the black church can make to gay men and lesbians, and to other relational refugees. This father was able to see his son's need to maintain his relationship with his biological family. He realized that his son was reaching out to him and others and that he had allowed his son's behavior to prevent this from happening. The father made up his mind that his son's needs were more important than the rule-oriented ethics of his denomination. He reached out to his son and healed the relationship that was broken. Reconciliation took place. He put aside his negative feelings and looked upon his son as a child of God. The son and his lover received the embrace they longed for as they faced death together. No doubt, the father also regretted all the time that had been lost because of the period of alienation between them. The father came to the realization that he allowed his beliefs about homosexuality to exclude his son from his love and that that was wrong.

From the perspective of pastoral counseling, the father models the benefits of a narrative theological orientation, combined with a shame psychological orientation. He recognized that his son was still a vital part of his family and God's family. He knew that the story of their relationship did not have to end in alienation or even because of death. Therefore, he reached out to his son and became reconciled. This man understood that God works out God's activity in concrete ways as life unfolds, as we join God in reaching out in love.

Psychologically, the father was able to look beyond his son's behavior and see his son's real need. His son needed to be loved and accepted by the family that gave him birth. He saw his son's need to be embraced by love, and he responded.

Homosexuals, as all human beings, need to know that they have a home where they are cared for and respected. A punitive, propositional, and guilt-oriented approach that isolates gays and lesbians from the village, the faith community, is inappropriate. Trying to change the behavior of gays and lesbians by excluding them from the community is not a helpful approach. The village and the church need to maintain the tension between the heterosexual norm for human sexual behavior and the embracing of homosexuals as a vital part of the community. Adopting dynamic, narrative-based ethical models and shame psychological approaches can help in this process.

Conclusion

It is a terrible fate to face death alone. The feeling of isolation is compounded when you are alienated from your support network because of your race, sexual orientation, or other immutable characteristic. Death is a time to be surrounded by a loving community, to feel a supportive and caring embrace. It is a time to face together with those you love the great questions of life's meaning and what lies beyond. Facing death, life seems sweeter, richer, more intense. Every moment is heightened. But this is true only if one is embraced, supported, and loved. There are many possibilities for living meaningful lives despite death's approach. The role of the village as a caring community is important in helping to actualize these possibilities. It is most important that no one die outside the gate, as a relational refugee.

The church is the Body of Christ. It is a community of believers, disciples, and pilgrims who live together in community and journey together toward God's coming kingdom. It is a place of refuge and hospitality where all are welcome and all give to those who are in need. It is a community of hospitality based on Jesus' own modeling behavior. The stranger, the prostitute, the tax collector, the leper, and the demoniac are all welcomed as members of this group, as recipients of grace, as guests at Jesus' table. Baptism incorporates all of these members, making those who once were far off a part of the Body. Members are then brought up in the faith, the lifestyle, and the narratives of this Body. Thereby, they become children of God in the midst of loving community.

This church, this Body, this hospitable and loving community is called to continue the work of hospitality in a world filled with relational refugees. Refugees need a home and the church is that home. The church needs to not only welcome those who show up on Sunday morning but also reach out to those who are alienated. As we have seen, relational refugees need special attention, for not only do they suffer from lack of community, but their ability to join community is also impaired. In addition, some relational refugees are alienated from family and other primary communities, and many are also alienated from the church itself and so are doubly difficult to reach and serve. For this reason, relational refugees pose a considerable challenge to the church, its members and ministers, and to theological education as an institution.

In this conclusion, key questions regarding the church and theological education will be examined. My concern is to enable the church to identify, reach out, and embrace the relational refugee. To this end, I discuss the fears and needs of relational refugees, models of church that address these needs, and finally, models of theological education that train those who can be mentors for relational refugees.

The Fears and Needs of Relational Refugees

Relational refugees have many fears about the church. Many are sensitive to the relational and emotional environment that exists. They fear the judgment that the church so often offers in place of hospitality and understanding. Because relational refugees hunger for relationships, they often pursue relationships and other activities that the churches have traditionally condemned. Because of their history of failed relationships, refugees are also particularly vulnerable to messages of rejection. Many feel shamed, embarrassed, and guilty about their behavior and attitudes and do not feel worthy of love or acceptance. Others have an uncomfortable truce with their alienated status and have given up any hope of ever being part of a loving and caring community.

There are many people inside and outside of our churches who are relational refugees and who feel alienated from vital relationships. Relational refugees share in common isolation from community. All refugees need to be reintegrated into nurturing relationships so that they can heal and grow. But there are as many reasons behind their predicament as there are refugees. Some are victims of abuse. Some are perpetrators of abuse and violence. Some are both perpetrators and victims at the same time. Some are recovering addicts and substance abusers. Some harbor deep secrets that are crippling their capacities for intimacy and community. Some have been hurt in families or communities where they suffered abuse, inadequate care, or rejection. Some are angry because they have been taken for granted, ignored, overlooked, and left out. Some feel abandoned and deserted. And some belong to groups that the powerful devalue and stigmatize.

The results of these various afflictions are common needs. Most relational refugees believe they are unlovable. They share a deep desire to be embraced and loved. Many have grown accustomed to having love withheld from them. They have experienced only conditional love, love offered only if they conformed to certain behaviors. Human love is conditional, only divine love is unmerited and all embracing. But refugees cannot allow themselves to feel unconditional love because they do not know what it is like. They are trapped between their need and desire for love and their conviction that they are not worthy of such love. Only God can truly free them from the trap, but the church must offer what it can. The church, at the very least, must remove itself as an obstacle to the experience of God for refugees. The church must dismantle its barriers and reach out.

It is true that the church is the Body of Christ, a community of love and hospitality. It is also true that the churches are broken groups of frail human beings who love but also hate, who welcome but also exclude. How can, then, the churches be places of unconditional love and care? Can churches be made up of a majority of people who are secure enough in themselves, in their own home-worlds, that they can welcome almost anyone? What the church needs today are members who are secure in their home-worlds so that they can reach out to help relational refugees reconnect. The church needs people who have found God's accepting hospitality and are, thereby, enabled to offer that same hospitality to others.

Building a Caring Environment

The propositional language of our ethics and doctrine alienates many relational refugees. The regulation of conduct through norms, rules, laws, and traditions is extremely important and necessary. Basing our approach to ministry and to people primarily on propositional doctrine and law, however, can be problematic for the relational refugee. Relational refugees are, for the most part, very aware of the doctrines, laws, and norms of churches. Those refugees who feel the most alienated from community may even have contempt for such approaches. Moreover, many relational refugees see the inconsistencies between the official pronouncements of church regarding appropriate lifestyle and behavioral choices for members and the actual conduct of church folk. I am not proposing that churches abandon propositional approaches to moral instruction, but rather that they balance their articulation and enforcement of rules with more dynamic approaches that invite people into the narratives on which the community is based.

The example of the early church is helpful as a model for how our communities can balance rules with stories. The first Christians were Jesus' friends. They met him in the flesh and came to believe. The first stage of community formation is experiential—an encounter with Jesus. Jesus told his friends stories—old ones from the Jewish scriptures and new ones. They walked with him on the way. After he died, rose, and ascended, they kept meeting, eating, telling stories. They also began to tell these stories to others. Their small group developed into many small groups. This is the second stage, a generation of those who had not met Jesus but heard about him from those who had known him. The third phase of faith community building came when those who were recruited into the faith community in the first two stages began, in turn, to reach out to others. At this stage, the communities are bigger. They need more regulation. The stories and traditions are also more numerous. New converts need more formal instruction. In all three stages what attracted converts to the faith was the behavior and story of those who believed that God's kingdom was coming and all were welcome to join in the celebration. This is what Jesus said to the disciples and what they said to the first households and what the early church said to the world. It was the vitality of the community and its shared narrative that attracted people. The rules came later.

As the early church grew, conflicts and misunderstandings erupted. These communities faced many of the behavioral and moral problems that we face today. People brought prior lives and commitments with them into the community that made it hard for them to adjust to new norms. The early church sought to conform itself to the mind of Christ through narrative but also through the enforcement of standards. It seems to me that the early church's struggle to bring the behavior of its members into line with Christ is instructive for us. The first generations of Christians used a combination of narrative and propositional approaches to form and shape people in faith communities. Paul emphasizes the values of hospitality and love in community building and shaping character.

He had high expectations regarding members' ethical behavior but these expectations were not divorced from the narrative context of those ethics. In his preaching and writing, Paul highlighted hospitality, tolerance, inclusivity, and high ethical standards as the foundational values of Christian community. Those who came after Paul, the Pauline school, began to divorce doctrine from narrative, emphasizing exclusive and hierarchical models of church. I contend that we need to recover the earlier forms of Christian community in which narrative shaped character, and hospitality, tolerance, and inclusivity were the dominant values.

Norms governing the behavior of the early church grew out of the faith communities' life together as they reflected on the life, death, and resurrection of Jesus Christ. The primary goal was to imitate the values by which Jesus lived and died. These norms were passed on from one generation to the next through their shared liturgical and religious life. It is our task to continue this passing on, this traditioning. However, it is not possible to pass on the traditions of the past without the necessary relational ingredients among community members. To be a community, to form ourselves into community members and pilgrims, we must first be together to share stories, meals, and values. The next level of character formation and community building is our communal reflections on our life together in light of the stories of faith that we remember. The third level of character and community formation is to form, out of these reflections, abstract norms and values that guide our behavioral choices and define our identity. In the order of things, the normative and propositional follow the formation of community through narrative. Today, relational refugees need to be approached on the first and second orders of character and community formation—the sharing of stories, and the gathering in fellowship. To begin our ministries at the propositional level is alienating to such persons. Outreach to relational refugees must emphasize hospitality and acceptance, not judgment and doctrine.

In communities that know the power of narrative to shape character, the emphasis is on welcoming people and helping them understand themselves within the unfolding of God's salvation story. The emphasis is on a holistic process of character formation within a supportive community that is itself undergoing formation as the Body of Christ. Norms are not lost, but are tied organically to the story rather than appearing in the abstract.

In most cases, relational refugees seek a community of hospitality where they can grow and develop in light of their own self-understanding. This is done best in those faith communities that are made up of people with the following characteristics. (1) They are secure in their emotional, relational, spiritual, and cognitive home. (2) They are emotionally mature in the sense that they know who they are, apart from others. (3) The congregation is multigenerational with a significant number of people who have successfully managed the midlife crisis and stand as reservoirs of wisdom and tradition. (4) There is significant cross-generational interaction. (5) People can reach out in hospitality without being threatened by those who are different. (6) Congregational leaders, including the pastor, are secure in their home-worlds, are self-differentiated, and have vital cross-generational connections.

These congregational and leadership characteristics are important because it is the fear of the unknown that prevents people from embracing those who might be different. The crucial vision for the leaders of congregations is to develop an accepting environment where people can feel at home and welcomed. This takes mature people who are deeply engaged in all aspects of the life of their faith communities.

Liturgy, or worship, deserves special attention because it is a source of energy for believers and an organizing center of the community's life. It is the regular, weekly work of the people on behalf of the world. It proclaims and embodies the central values of the faith. Hospitality grows out of the liturgical centering of the congregation. Without this centering, a congregation cannot create a viable inclusive and relational environment.

Training Leaders for Vital Congregations

My attention now turns to how theological seminaries can best train leaders who can be mentors for relational refugees and who can help congregations become vital centers of hospitality. Just as vital congregations are made up of people who are mature, self-differentiated, at home in the world, who extend hospitality, and form vital, caring environments, it appears to me that seminaries need to also be about forming individuals with these characteristics. But this will require some changes in how we go about the task of theological education.

For a long time seminaries have been introducing seminarians to different worlds, both ancient and modern. For some, the seminary experience is unsettling, faith shaking. While this process of shaking up the world of the seminary student is important, the need to help the theological student find his or her home in a faith world is also important. The work of the seminary is not done when students have developed a healthy view of the complexity of the world and when they have developed critical and analytical abilities. The seminary must also participate in the forming of theological students into spiritual guides who can help mentor people and congregations.

It seems to me that theological education needs to be about providing an instructional environment where full-time and part-time faculty, administration, and staff can be mentors for theological students. What I mean by mentoring is not simply serving as a role model. To me, mentoring involves four crucial dimensions: attitude internalization, plot identification, role participation, and scene re-creation. The instructional dimensions of the curriculum should create opportunities for instructors to mentor students on all four of these levels.

Theological education should be about mentoring students in such a way that they will also become mentors. At the end of three years of theological education, students should have: a comfortable grasp of their calling, identified the faith and behavioral science traditions that inform that calling, and encountered among faculty, peers, staff, administrators, and field teachers significant mentors who can help them critically and constructively go about their own unique ministry.

This book opened with the identification of an indigenous model of knowing, teaching, and learning, based on copying, or mimesis. This process of mentoring occurs through copying attitudes, constructing positive scenes for growth, internalizing meaningful roles, and discovering positive plots for engaging life. Mentoring can occur both formally, in practicums, and informally, in various personal relationships. The formal aspects are those who are the designated instructors whose task is to help students find their theological and ministerial home. The informal aspects are those who carry out the task of helping students find their theological and ministerial homes when they have not been given the task formally. I taught at Garrett-Evangelical Theological Seminary between 1985–1991. At that time, there were about thirty students, four faculty, one administrator, and many support staff members who were African American. The rest of the seminary community was predominantly Euro-American with small numbers of Hispanic, Asian, African, and international students. In the African American community, the most influential person in the formation of students was not a faculty member or administrator, but the head of maintenance, a man named Charlie Underwood. Mr. Underwood was a deacon in a local black church. He was secure in his world, the world of faith and ministry. He watched students and their ways of interacting within the seminary community and the surrounding community. He also understood the meaning of ministry and what the church needed from its ministers. He had superior relationship skills and was able to win the confidence of students. When he retired, many students and alumni hailed him as the single most influential person in their seminary careers.

The importance of Mr. Underwood in the life of students at Garrett-Evangelical illustrates what I mean by a village understanding of the ministerial process. There are many dynamic factors that help a seminarian become an effective church leader, preacher, and mentor. In many cases, the informal instructors are just as important as the formal instructors. It is important to think of preparing mentors as a total community task. Seminary curricula should recognize and integrate these informal relationships, and people with whom the students come into contact daily, into the overall education program. In the small African village, the elders, whether part of one's immediate family or not, were the mentors. Older brothers, aunts, uncles, cousins, and a host of other community people made up the instructional curriculum. The same is true for theological education, and we should count such persons as part of the instructional staff.

It takes a village to develop a prospective theological student into a mentor. In fact, becoming a mentor is a lifelong process in which seminary is only a small part. As faculty, we need to get over the feeling that we are the essential ingredient in the formation of ministers. Rather, we should embrace the variety of ways of learning and the critical role of informal instructors to relieve us of the full burden of the educational task. The curriculum consists of anything and everything that helps us accomplish our goals. Within the theological community and those auxiliary communities with which our students come into contact, there are a number of mentors on whom our students can draw and receive what they need in order to become better persons and mentors themselves.

As mentors, aware of the predicament of relational refugees, operating at the level of narrative and mimesis, rather than proposition, and offering hospitality and the good news of unconditional love, ministers of the gospel can begin to reconstruct the village that reflects the values of the kingdom of God. The church needs such leaders. The world needs such people. Relational refugees await a word of welcome so that they can return home.

NOTES

Foreword

1. James Baldwin, "The Discovery of What It Means to Be an American," *New York Times Book Review* (January 25, 1959).

Preface

1. Archie Smith, Jr., *Navigating the Deep River: Spirituality in African American Families* (Cleveland: United Church Press, 1997).

Introduction

1. Peter L. Berger, *Facing Up to Modernity: Excursions in Society, Politics, and Religion* (New York: BasicBooks, 1977), p. 70.

2. Archie Smith, Jr., *Navigating the Deep River: Spirituality in African American Families* (Cleveland: United Church Press, 1997), p. 36.

3. For a discussion of the concept of emotional cut off see Edward P. Wimberly, *Counseling African American Marriages and Families* (Louisville: Westminster John Knox Press, 1997), pp. 41-43.

4. The concept of the emotional refugee also grows out of the sociology of knowledge in the work of Peter Berger, Brigitte Berger, and Hansfried Kellner. See *The Homeless Mind: Modernization and Conciousness* (New York: Random House, 1974). In this book, they conceptualize the homeless mind as one that has developed as the result of the introduction of multiple ways of understanding reality, and this puts pressure on the individual to have to choose from a variety of competing possibilities. One such image is that of a machine, where the person envisages herself or himself as a component part of a machine rather than as a member of a community with a past. See pages 26-37.

5. See Smith, *Navigating the Deep River*, for a discussion of these values.

6. For a disussion of violence as a means of redemption in North American society see Robert Jewett, *St. Paul Returns to the Movies: Triumph Over Shame* (Grand Rapids: Eerdmans, 1998).

7. Audre Lorde, *Sister Outsider: Essays and Speeches* (Trumansburg, New York: The Crossing Press, 1984), p. 112.

1. A Model for Pastoral Care:
African American Mentoring

1. See Robert Franklin, *Another Days Journey* (Cleveland: United Church Press, 1997).

2. See Edward P. Wimberly, "Indigenous Theological Reflection on Pastoral Supervision: An African American Perspective," *Journal of Supervision and Training in Ministry* 13 (1991): 180-89.

3. See Romney Moseley, *Becoming a Self Before God: Critical Transformations* (Nashville: Abingdon Press, 1991); and Archie Smith, Jr., *Navigating the Deep River: Spirituality in African American Families* (Cleveland: United Church Press, 1997).

4. See Archie Smith, Jr., *Navigating the Deep River*, p. 32.

5. I draw on a modern theory of mimetic reflection rooted primarily in the thinking of William Schweiker. He plumbs the work of Hans Gadamer and Paul Ricoeur for their understanding of the basic process of meaning making and thinking in his work. His conclusion is that we learn through the processes of mimicking or copying plots and engaging in role performance. See William Schweiker, *Mimetic Reflections: A Study in Hermeneutics, Theology, and Ethics* (New York: Fordham University Press, 1990).

6. These ideas were influenced by the work of Catherine Bell expressed in *Ritual Theory and Ritual Practice* (New York: Oxford University Press, 1992), pp. 109-16.

7. See J. Paul Sampley, *Walking Between the Times* (Minneapolis: Fortress, 1991), p. 22. Here Sampley explores the idea that Paul's worldview expected people to grow and to mature. Life in Christ was a growth process.

8. Ibid., pp. 87-90.

9. Modernity is critical of the fact that the dominant images of what it means to be human have been based on European and American men. The philosophical traditions of the past have focused on universal issues that have ignored the particular characteristics and experiences of those who were at the margins, on the periphery, and on the bottom. The experiences of African Americans and women were systematically excluded from the voices that made up the universal. The impact of this exclusion is now the subject of many books. Consequently, postmodern thought is about redefining what it means to be human and how to make meaning in ways that give expression to the left out voices.

2. Violence and the Relational Refugee

1. Edward P. Wimberly, *Counseling African American Marriages and Families* (Louisville: Westminster John Knox Press, 1997), p. 112.

2. Robert Jewett, *Saint Paul Returns to the Movies: Triumph over Shame* (Grand Rapids: Eerdmans, 1998).

3. For a discussion of contemporary shame and its impact, see Edward P. Wimberly, *Recovering From Shame: Preaching and Pastoral Counseling* (Nashville: Abingdon Press, 1998).

4. Robert Franklin, "Travelin' Shoes: Resources for Our Journey," *The Journal of the Interdenominational Theological Center* (fall 1997): 3.

3. Animosity in Intimate Relationships and the
Relational Refugee

1. Toni Morrison, *The Bluest Eye* (New York: Plume, 1994), p. 42.

2. Alice Walker, *The Color Purple* (New York: Washington Square Press, 1982), p. 124.

3. I mention a few resources on counseling with and preaching to African American married couples. For counselors: Archie Smith, Jr., *Navigating the Deep River: Spirituality in African American Families* (Cleveland: United Church Press, 1997); Clarence Walker, *Bibical Counseling with African-Americans: Taking a Ride in the Ethiopian's Chariot* (Grand Rapids: Zondervan Publishing House, 1992); and Edward P. Wimberly, *Counseling African American Marriages and Families* (Louisville: Westminster John Knox Press, 1997). And, for preachers:

Renita Weems, *I Ask for Intimacy: Stories of Blessings, Betrayals and Birthings* (San Diego: LuraMedia, 1993); and Jeremiah Wright, *Good News: Sermons of Hope for Today's Families* (Valley Forge: Judson, 1995).

4. Adolescence and the Relational Refugee

1. For a discussion of black identity and negative identity formation in the work of Erik Erikson, see Edward P. Wimberly, *Counseling African American Marriages and Families* (Louisville: Westminster John Knox Press, 1997), p. 54.

2. Toni Morrison, *The Bluest Eye* (New York: Plume, 1994), p. 20.

3. Ibid., p. 38.

4. Ibid., p. 39.

5. Ibid., p. 47.

6. See, as an example, Emilie Townes, *A Troubling in My Soul: Womanist Perspectives on Evil and Suffering* (Maryknoll, New York: Orbis Books, 1993), pp. 1-9.

7. On the historical development of racism in the West, see Cornel West, *Prophetic Fragments* (Grand Rapids: Eerdmans, 1998), pp. 97-108.

8. See Archie Smith, Jr., *Navigating the Deep River: Spirituality in African American Families* (Cleveland: United Church Press, 1997), p. 23.

9. Hymn lyrics from James Weldon Johnson, "Lift Every Voice and Sing" (Edward B. Marks Music Company, 1921).

10. Archie Smith, Jr., *Navigating the Deep River*, p. 24.

11. See "30 years after Kerner report, some say racial divide wider" CNN U.S. News Story Page, March 1, 1998. (www.cnn.com/US/9803/01/Kerner.commission/)

12. See Archie Smith, Jr., *Navigating the Deep River*, pp. 26-27.

5. Poverty, Prosperity, and the Relational Refugee

1. Lorraine Hansberry, *A Raisin in the Sun* (New York: Vintage Books, 1994).

2. Andrew Billingsley, *Climbing Jacob's Ladder: The Enduring Legacy of African-American Families* (New York: Simon & Schuster, 1992), p. 224.

3. See Edward P. Wimberly, *African American Pastoral Care* (Nashville: Abingdon Press, 1991), pp. 12-17; See also Henry Mitchell and Nicholas Lewter, *Soul Theology* (New York: Harper & Row, 1986), p. 11; Archie Smith, Jr., *Navigating the Deep River: Spirituality in African American Families* (Cleveland: United Church Press, 1997), p. 94.

4. Hansberry, *A Raisin in the Sun*, p. 145.

5. Smith, *Navigating the Deep River: Spirituality in African American Families*, p. 20.

6. Ibid., p. 33.

7. William Oliver, *The Violent Social World of Black Men* (New York: Lexington Books, 1994), p. 10.

6. Grandparenting and the Relational Refugee

1. Andrew Billingsley has documented the system of both informal and formal adoptions within African American family systems in his *Climbing Jacob's Ladder: The Enduring Legacy of African-American Families* (New York: Simon & Schuster, 1992).

2. Don Browning, *Religious Thought and Modern Psychologies: A Critical Conversation in Theology of Culture* (Philadelphia: Fortress Press, 1988), pp. 224-25.

3. See Thomas Banks, "The Third Life of Grange Copeland," in *Masterpieces of African-American Literature*, Frank N. Masill, editor (New York: HarperCollins, 1992), pp. 573-76.

4. Archie Smith, Jr., *Navigating the Deep River: Spirituality in African American Families* (Cleveland: United Church Press, 1997), p. xxviii.

5. Ibid.

6. Ibid.

7. Drug Addiction, Surrogate Fathers, and the Relational Refugee

1. Alice Childress, *A Hero Ain't Nothin' But a Sandwich* (New York: Coward, McCann & Geoghegan, Inc., 1973).

2. Andrew Billingsley, *Climbing Jacob's Ladder: The Enduring Legacy of African-American Families* (New York: Simon & Schuster, 1992).

3. Don Browning, *Religious Thought and Modern Psychologies: A Critical Conversation in Theology and Culture* (Philadelphia: Fortress Press, 1988), pp. 224-25.

4. Alice Childress, *A Hero Ain't Nothin' But a Sandwich*, p. 73.

5. Ibid., p. 69.

6. Ibid., p. 30.

7. Ibid.

8. Grant S. Shockley concludes that black churches have never reached more than a minority of black youth. See "Christian Education and the Black Church: A Contextual Approach," *The Journal of the Interdenominational Theological Center* (spring 1975): 85.

9. Edward P. Wimberly, *A Conceptual Model for Pastoral Care in the Black Church Utilizing Systems and Crisis Theories* (Boston University Graduate School, 1976); see also *Pastoral Care in the Black Church* (Nashville: Abingdon Press, 1979).

10. See Rod Hunter, "The Power of God unto Salvation: Transformative Ecclesia and the Renewal of Pastoral Counseling," *The Journal of the Interdenominational Theological Center* (winter-spring 1998).

11. Edward P. Wimberly, *Pastoral Counseling and Spiritual Values: A Black Point of View* (Nashville: Abingdon, 1982), p. 73.

12. Ibid., p. 9.

13. Ibid., p. 14.

14. Ibid., p. 76.

15. Important resources for this include Edward P. Wimberly, *Counseling African American Marriages and Families* (Louisville: Westminster John Knox Press, 1997); Nancy Boyd Franklin, *Black Families in Therapy: A Multisystems Approach* (New York: Guilford Press, 1989); and Archie Smith, Jr., *Navigating the Deep River: Spirituality in African American Families* (Cleveland: United Church Press, 1997).

16. For an account of this program see John Leland, "Savior of the Streets," *Newsweek* (June 1, 1998): 20-25.

17. Ibid., p. 22.

18. Ibid., p. 20.

8. Dying with Dignity and the Relational Refugee

1. Ernest Becker, *The Denial of Death* (New York: The Free Press, 1973).

2. The two stories are found in the following books. The first story of AIDS is found in a book written by Earl E. Shelp, Ronald H. Sunderland, and Peter W. A. Mansell entitled *AIDS: Personal Stories in Pastoral Perspective* (New York: Pilgrim Press, 1986), pp. 99-105. The second story is a novel written by Ernest J. Gaines, *A Lesson Before Dying* (New York: Vintage Contemporaries, 1993).

3. Archie Smith, Jr., *Navigating the Deep River: Spirituality in African American Families* (Cleveland: United Church Press, 1997), p. 38.

4. Ernest J. Gaines, *A Lesson Before Dying*, p. 223.

5. Ibid., pp. 230-31.

6. Ibid., p. 230.

7. Ibid., p. 231.

8. Ibid., p. 83.

9. Ibid., pp. 253-54.

10. Edward P. Wimberly, *Pastoral Counseling and Spiritual Values: A Black Point of View* (Nashville: Abingdon, 1982), p. 88.

11. For a detailed account of how communities of faith and their stories help to shape the character of people, see Stanley Hauerwas, *A Community of Character: Toward a Constructive Christian Social Ethic* (Notre Dame: University of Notre Dame Press, 1981), pp. 1-88.

12. For a contrast between narrative and propositional ways of shaping truth, see George Lindbeck, *The Nature of Doctrine: Religion and Theology in a Postliberal Age* (Philadelphia: Westminster Press, 1984), pp. 16-19.

13. This position that accepts the homosexual as a church member but deems homosexual practice to be inconsistent with the faith is very similar to the stance stated in *The Book of Discipline of The United Methodist Church* (Nashville: The United Methodist Publishing House, 1996), p. 89.

14. Smith, *Navigating the Deep River: Spirituality in African American Families*, p. 38.

15. See Larry Kent Graham, *Discovering Images of God: Narratives of Care Among Lesbians and Gays* (Louisville: Westminster John Knox, 1997), p. 45.

16. Shelp, Sunderland, and Mansell, *AIDS*, pp. 99-105.

135

LaVergne, TN USA
01 September 2009
156546LV00004B/75/A

5370426R0

Made in the USA
Lexington, KY
02 May 2010